OLD TESTAMENT SURVEY

OLD TESTAMENT SURVEY

REVISED EDITION

By
KEVIN CONNER & KEN MALMIN

Distributed By:
Bible Temple Publications
7545 N.E. Glisan Street
Portland, Oregon 97213

ISBN 0-914936-21-2
PRINTED IN U.S.A.

INTRODUCTION

It is of utmost importance that the Bible student obtain a good grasp of the Bible as a whole. However, in order to do so he must first gain an understanding of each book that makes up The Book. This text has been designed to be of help in this process of understanding the parts and relating them to the whole.

Old

The format of this book is quite simple. It is designed to give a patterned glimpse of each book of the New Testament. This has been done by applying these ten points to each book: (1) Titles, (2) Author, (3) Date, (4) Key Words and Phrases, (5) Key Verses, (6) Purpose, (7) Message, (8) Outline, (9) Summary, and (10) Christ Seen. The following is an explanation of each of the ten points.

1. TITLES:

Under this heading you will find basically three things: First, the meaning of the title of the book is given (e.g. Genesis means "in the beginning"). Next, significant titles given to the book by Hebrew manuscripts or the Septuagint, as well as alternate titles, are listed. Last, a distinct title has been suggested for each book. This title is meant to both describe the content of the book and to distinguish it from the other books of the Bible (e.g. Genesis is called The Book of Beginnings because it presents the beginning of all things relating to creation and redemption).

2. AUTHOR:

Under this heading is listed the author of the book. In cases where the book does not name its author, the most probable author from our point of view has been given. In the Prophetical books you will also find a descriptive title of that prophet's ministry, (e.g. Isaiah is called "The Prophet of Redemption") and a reference as to whom he ministered.

3. DATE:

Under this heading you will find first under the historical books a reference to the number of years that pass during the accounts given in the book and under the prophetical books the number of years the prophet ministered along with the names of the kings that reigned during the time of his ministry. Then for every book an approximate date has been given as to when the book was written. (There is a great diversity of opinion in the field of Old Testament chronology and we do not claim to be authorities in these matters. The dates included in this text were considered to be conservative estimates.)

4. KEY WORDS AND PHRASES:

Under this heading you will find words and phrases that are keys to understanding the book at hand. These have been chosen on the basis of frequency of usage, relation to the subject of the book, and frequency of usage in relation to usage in other books of the Bible. These tabulations are based upon the King James Version unless otherwise noted. These words can be used for good word/theme studies in their respective books.

5. KEY VERSES:

Under this heading you will find verses that express the main subject, theme, or message of the book.

6. PURPOSE:

Under this heading you will find statements that answer the question, "Why was this book written?". These lend insight into the importance of each book. It must be considered that there are many different types of reasons why a book is written (e.g. for historical, instructional, prophetical, etc. reasons). Those thought most important have been included.

7. MESSAGE:

Under this heading you will find, with some exceptions, the statements of principle that are taught by each book as a whole or at least by a major portion of it. Of these sort of statements there could be no end but once again only those felt most significant have been included.

8. OUTLINE:

Under this heading you will find a brief, condensed outline of each book showing its structure and arrangement.

9. SUMMARY:

Under this heading you will find a paragraph description of the book, pointing out its subject and its relation to other books of the Bible, as well as other facts of interest concerning the book or its author.

10. CHRIST SEEN:

Under this heading you will find a brief description of some ways in which Christ can be seen in the book (through types, prophecies, etc.) along with Scripture references supporting them.

Any correspondence concerning this text may be directed to:

Ken Malmin
Portland Bible College
9201 N.E. Fremont
Portland, Oregon 97220
U.S.A.

THE BOOKS OF THE OLD TESTAMENT

#	Book	The Book Of:
1.	GENESIS	Beginnings
2.	EXODUS	Redemption
3.	LEVITICUS	Approach
4.	NUMBERS	Wanderings
5.	DEUTERONOMY	Remembrance
6.	JOSHUA	Conquest
7.	JUDGES	Failure through Compromise
8.	RUTH	Grace
9.	I SAMUEL	The Transition
10.	II SAMUEL	The King
11.	I KINGS	The Disruption
12.	II KINGS	The Dispersion
13.	I CHRONICLES	The Theocracy
14.	II CHRONICLES	Relapse and Reformation
15.	EZRA	Restoration
16.	NEHEMIAH	Reconstruction
17.	ESTHER	Providence
18.	JOB	Blessing through Suffering
19.	PSALMS	Prayer and Praise
20.	PROVERBS	Wisdom
21.	ECCLESIASTES	Human Wisdom
22.	SONG OF SOLOMON	Love
23.	ISAIAH	Salvation
24.	JEREMIAH	The Backslider
25.	LAMENTATIONS	Mourning
26.	EZEKIEL	Visions
27.	DANIEL	The Kingdoms
28.	HOSEA	Law and Love
29.	JOEL	The Day of the Lord
30.	AMOS	Punishment
31.	OBADIAH	Retribution
32.	JONAH	Mercy on the Gentiles
33.	MICAH	Conviction
34.	NAHUM	Vengeance
35.	HABAKKUK	Faith
36.	ZEPHANIAH	The Day of Wrath
37.	HAGGAI	The Rebuilding of the Temple
38.	ZECHARIAH	Messianic Visions
39.	MALACHI	The Lord's Messengers

THE BOOKS OF THE OLD TESTAMENT

THE LAW	HISTORY 17	PENTATEUCH 5	HISTORICAL PENTATEUCH 5	GENESIS EXODUS LEVITICUS NUMBERS DEUTERONOMY
		HISTORICAL BOOKS 12	PRE-EXILE HISTORY 9	JOSHUA JUDGES RUTH I SAMUEL II SAMUEL I KINGS II KINGS I CHRONICLES II CHRONICLES
			POST-EXILE HISTORY 3	EZRA NEHEMIAH ESTHER
THE PSALMS	POETRY 5	POETICAL BOOKS 5	POETRY (THE HEART) 5	JOB PSALMS PROVERBS ECCLESIASTES SONG OF SOLOMON
THE PROPHETS	PROPHECY 17	MAJOR PROPHETS 5	PROPHETICAL PENTATEUCH 5	ISAIAH JEREMIAH LAMENTATIONS EZEKIEL DANIEL
		MINOR PROPHETS 12	PRE-EXILE PROPHECY 9	HOSEA JOEL AMOS OBADIAH JONAH MICAH NAHUM HABAKKUK ZEPHANIAH
			POST-EXILE PROPHECY 3	HAGGAI ZECHARIAH MALACHI

GENESIS

1. **TITLES:**

    A. Genesis = in the beginning, origin, births
    B. The Book of Beginnings

2. **AUTHOR:**

    Written by Moses, who also wrote Exodus, Leviticus, Numbers, and Deuteronomy. These five books make up the Pentateuch which was called "The Law of Moses" or "The Book of Moses" in the New Testament (Lk. 24:27, 44; Acts 28:23).

3. **DATE:**

    A. Covers approximately 2400 years from Adam to Joseph.
    B. Written about 1440 B.C.

4. **KEY WORDS:**

    A. Begat --- 67   *after His kind*   *17*
    B. Seed --- 58
    C. Generation (s) -- 21
    D. Begin (an, ing) --- 12

5. **KEY VERSES:** 1:1; 3:15

6. **PURPOSE:**

    A. To give an account of the origin of all things.
    B. To show God as the originator of creation and redemption.
    C. To show the origin of all nations and the choice of the Hebrew nation as God's peculiar people from whom the Redeemer would come.

7. **MESSAGE:**

    A. It is necessary for man to know by failure his own weakness and insufficiency, before he will voluntarily choose God.
    B. Under every condition the failure of man is met by the salvation of God.

8. **OUTLINE:**

    I.   The Beginnings of the Universe and Man . . . . Ch. 1-11
         Four Outstanding Events;
                 Creation/Fall/Flood/Babel --------   All Nations
    II. The Beginnings of the Hebrew Nation . . . . Ch. 12-50
         Four Outstanding Persons;
                 Abraham/Isaac/Jacob/Joseph ----   Chosen Nation

9. **SUMMARY:**

    Genesis is the "seed-book" of the whole Bible, the source of all the streams of truth that run through all the Scripture and consummate in the Book of Revelation. Genesis and Revelation are the beginning and ending of all things pertaining to creation and redemption. Genesis gives us the beginning of: the universe (1:1), man (1:26, 27), marriage (2:21-24), sin (3:1-7), blood-sacrifice (3:21; 4:1-7), nations (10:32), the Hebrew nation (12:2), and the covenants of redemption (3:15; 17:7).   *13:15*

10. **CHRIST SEEN:**   *Christ the blood sacrifice Gen 3:21*

    Christ is seen as the Creator (Gen. 1; Col. 1:16), the Beginning (Rev. 1:8), "The Seed of the woman" (Gen. 3:15; Mt. 1:23), the Ark of Salvation (Gen. 6-8; Lk. 2:30), our Isaac; the Only Begotten Son (Jn. 3:16), and our Joseph; the Beloved Son (Mt. 3:17). Christ is also seen in numerous other types throughout the book.

EXODUS

1. **TITLES:**

    A. Exodus = the going out, departure
    B. "These Are The Names" -- Hebrew Title (1:1)
    C. The Book of Redemption

2. **AUTHOR:**

    Written by Moses (Refer to Genesis).

3. **DATE:**

    A. Covers approximately 215 years, from the going of Jacob's family to Egypt to the giving of the law at Mount Sinai.
    B. Written between 1440 and 1400 B.C.

4. **KEY WORDS:**

A.	Moses	290	D.	Command (ed, eth, ment)	60
B.	Aaron ('s)	116	E.	Redeem (ed)	10
C.	Tabernacle	91	F.	Law (s)	7

5. **KEY VERSES:**   3:8; 19:3-6

6. **PURPOSE:**

    A. To show the beginning of the fulfillment of the Abrahamic Covenant.
    B. To show the redemption of the Hebrew nation in their deliverance from Egypt.
    C. To introduce the Mosaic Covenant, with its Moral, Civil and Ceremonial Law.

7. **MESSAGE:**

    A. God's redeeming grace is revealed to those who believe and obey.
    B. God desires to dwell among His redeemed people, but can only do so on His terms.

8. **OUTLINE:**

    I.   The Exodus ----------- The Power of God . . . . Ch. 1-18 (Historical)
    II. The Law -------------- The Holiness of God . . . . Ch. 19-24 (Moral/Civil)
    III. The Tabernacle ----- The Wisdom of God . . . . Ch. 25-40 (Ceremonial)

9. **SUMMARY:**

    Between Genesis and Exodus Israel had become a nation while in Egypt. The book opens with the nation's bondage there (Ch. 1) and the preparation of Moses to be their deliverer and mediator (Ch. 2-4). The book then continues with God's supernatural judgment upon Egypt by plagues and the redemption of Israel by the blood of the passover lamb (Ch. 5-12). Then as they headed toward the promised land (Abrahamic Covenant) they received at Mount Sinai, the Law (Mosaic Covenant), which included the Ten Commandments, the Civil Laws and the Ceremonial Laws (Ch. 13-24). The Ceremonial Law included the Tabernacle, the Priesthood and the Sacrifices. The book closes with the Glory of God coming to dwell in the midst of a redeemed people (Ch. 25-40).

10. **CHRIST SEEN:**

    Christ is seen as our Deliverer (Acts 5:31), Mediator (Heb. 8:6) and Lawgiver (Heb. 8:10) -- (Moses); as our High Priest (Heb. 2:17) -- (Aaron), our Passover Lamb (Ex. 12; Cor. 5:7) and as the Tabernacle of God with men (Ex. 25-40; Jn. 1:14).

LEVITICUS

1. **TITLES:**

    A. Leviticus = that which pertains to Levi.
    B. "And He Called" -- Hebrew Title (1:1)
    C. "The Levitical Book" -- Septuagint Title
    D. The Book of Worship
    E. The Book of Approach

2. **AUTHOR:**

    Written by Moses (Refer to Genesis).

3. **DATE:**

    A. Covers approximately one month; the first month of the second year after Israel came out of Egypt.
    B. Written about 1439 B.C.

4. **KEY WORDS:**

    A. Offering (293), Sacrifice (45), Oblation (10) ------------------------------------- 348
    B. Priest (s) -- 194
    C. Clean (46), Unclean (129) --- 175
    D. Holy (94), Sanctify (23), Sanctuary (12), Hallow (8) ------------------------- 137
        (Same Hebrew Root)
    E. Blood --- 88
    F. Atonement -- 49
    G. Redeem (ed, tion) --- 30

5. **KEY VERSE:** 19:2

6. **PURPOSE:**

    A. To give to Israel their proper approach to God.
    B. To instruct the priests concerning their ministry of offering sacrifices and oblations.
    C. To give distinction between the clean and the unclean.

7. **MESSAGE:**

    A. God is holy.
    B. Approach to God is only through a mediating priest offering a blood-sacrifice for atonement.

8. **OUTLINE:**

    I. The Way to God Through Sacrifice . . . . Ch. 1-16
        Offerings/Priesthood/Purifications
    II. The Walk With God Through Separation . . . . Ch. 17-27
        People/Priests/Feasts/Land

9. **SUMMARY:**

    In Genesis we see man ruined, in Exodus we see man redeemed, and in Leviticus we see man worshipping. In Genesis we see the man of worship, in Exodus we see the place of worship, and in Leviticus we see the manner of worship. In Exodus the Tabernacle is described and constructed while in Leviticus the prescribed offerings and the ministry of the priesthood is introduced and outlined (Lev. 1-10). Next the laws and regulations governing every area of the life of the people and priests are given. These laws related to their life spiritually, morally, physically, and ceremonially (Lev. 11-22). The book concludes by giving the laws pertaining to their religious observances such as Passover, Pentecost, Tabernacles, Sabbaths, and Jubilee years, as well as vows, tithes, and offerings (Lev. 23-27).

10. **CHRIST SEEN:**

    Christ is seen as our Sacrifice and Oblation (Heb. 10:12), our Holy High Priest (Heb. 7:26), making Atonement with His Blood for our sin (Heb. 9:14), and thus being our Way of Approach to God (Heb. 7:25).

NUMBERS

1. **TITLES:**

   A. Numbers = numbering the people
   B. "In the Wilderness" -- Hebrew Title (1:1)
   C. The Book of Wanderings

2. **AUTHOR:**

   Written by Moses (Refer to Genesis).

3. **DATE:**

   A. Covers a little less than 40 years, from Mt. Sinai to Jordan.
   B. Written about 1401 B.C.

4. **KEY WORDS:**

A.	Offering (s)	278	E.	Sanctuary	32
B.	Tabernacle	107	F.	Depart (ed)	27
C.	Pitch (ed)	49	G.	Remove (d)	23
D.	Wilderness	45	H.	Encamp (ed)	18

5. **KEY VERSES:** 14:28-34

6. **PURPOSE:**

   A. To give an account of the 40 years that Israel wandered in the Wilderness.
   B. To record the two numberings of the two generations at the beginning and ending of the 40 years.

7. **MESSAGE:**

   A. God's people are redeemed to serve.
   B. When God's people do not enter into God's promised rest it is due to unbelief and disobedience.
   C. God will always raise up a believing generation to inherit His Covenant-promises.

8. **OUTLINE:**

   I. The Old Generation - Sinai to Kadesh . . . . Ch. 1-14
         The First Numbering
   II. The Wandering - In the Wilderness . . . . Ch. 15-20
         The Transition
   III. The New Generation - Kadesh to Jordan . . . . Ch. 21-36
         The Second Numbering

9. **SUMMARY:**

   After receiving the Law, as seen in Exodus and Leviticus, and being numbered at Mt. Sinai, the old generation came to Kadesh - Barnea, the gateway to the promised land. There they rejected through unbelief the land promised to them in the Abrahamic Covenant. Because of their sin of unbelief they were caused to wander and perish in the wilderness, thus knowing God's breach of promise. In faithfulness to His Covenant, God raised up a new believing generation and prepared them for entering into the land.

10. **CHRIST SEEN:**

   Christ is seen as The Tabernacle (Jn. 1:14), our Sanctuary in the Wilderness (Ezek. 11:16), The Nazarite (Heb. 7:26), the Son of Man lifted up as the Serpent of Brass (Jn. 3:14), the Smitten Rock (I Cor. 10:4), and The "Star Out of Jacob" (Mt. 2:2).

DEUTERONOMY

1. **TITLES:**

   A. Deuteronomy = second law
   B. "These Are The Words" -- Hebrew Title (1:1)
   C. "Second Law" -- Septuagint Title
   D. The Book of Remembrance

2. **AUTHOR:**

   Written by Moses (1:1; 31:9, 22, 24-27) (Refer to Genesis).

3. **DATE:**

   A. Covers approximately two months (Deut. 1:3; 34:5, 8; Josh. 4:19). It also contains a review of the entire wanderings.
   B. Written about 1400 B.C.

4. **KEY WORDS:**

   A. Do, Keep, Observe (Two Hebrew Words) ---------------- 164
   B. Hear (d, ken) --- 69
   C. Heart (s) --- 49
   D. Love (d, th) -- 22
   E. Remember (ance) --- 16

5. **KEY VERSES:** 10:12, 13

6. **PURPOSE:**

   A. To remind Israel of their need to be faithful to the Covenant that God had made with them.
   B. To prepare Israel for entering, conquering, and possessing the promised land.

7. **MESSAGE:**

   A. Love for God is the proper motivation for obeying His laws.
   B. God requires His children to both hear and obey His commands.
   C. Those who obey are blessed, but those who disobey are cursed.

8. **OUTLINE:**

   I. Rejection of the Abrahamic Covenant . . . . Ch. 1-4   (Historical)
   II. Review of the Mosaic Covenant . . . . Ch. 4-26   (Legal)
      A. Moral Law . . . . Ch. 4-11
      B. Ceremonial Law . . . . Ch. 12-16
      C. Civil Law . . . . .Ch. 17-26
   III. Requirements of the Palestinian Covenant . . . . Ch. 27-34   (Prophetical)

9. **SUMMARY:**

   Deuteronomy is a review of the past with an eye to the future. It involves Israel's relationship to the Abrahamic, Mosaic, and Palestinian Covenants. The generation that had come out of Egypt had rejected the land as promised in the Abrahamic Covenant, and had died in the wilderness. Now the new generation coming out of the wilderness into that land is given the conditions of obtaining and maintaining it in the Mosaic and Palestinian Covenants.

   NOTE: Consider Christ's use of this book against Satan (Mt. 4:1-11; Deut. 6:13, 16; 8:3; 10:20). Christ quoted from this book more than any other Old Testament book.

10. **CHRIST SEEN:**

   Christ is seen as The True Prophet (Deut. 18:15-19; Acts 3:22), and our Rock (Deut. 32:4, 18, 31; I Cor. 10:4).

JOSHUA

1. **TITLES:**

    A. Joshua = Jehovah is salvation
    B. The Book of Conquest

2. **AUTHOR:**

    Written by Joshua (18:9; 24:25, 26).

3. **DATE:**

    A. Covers approximately 30 years, from the death of Moses to the death of Joshua.
    B. Written between 1390 and 1370 B.C.

4. **KEY WORDS:**

    A. Inherit (ance) -- 61
    B. Possess (ion) -- 24

5. **KEY VERSES:** 11:23; 21:43-45

6. **PURPOSE:**

    A. To show the fulfillment of God's promises in the giving of the promised land to Israel (23:14).
    B. To show how Israel failed to fully possess the land (18:3).

7. **MESSAGE:**

    A. God is faithful to keep His Covenant (Abrahamic) by giving the "Land" to the "Seed".
    B. Those who believe must labor to enter into all that God gives (Heb. 4).

8. **OUTLINE:**

    I.   Entering the Land . . . . Ch. 1-5
    II.   Conquering the Land . . . . Ch. 6-12
    III. Dividing the Land . . . . Ch. 13-22
    IV.   Farewell and Burial in the Land . . . . Ch. 23, 24

9. **SUMMARY:**

    The focal point of this book is clearly the promised land. It contains the accounts of how Israel entered, conquered and divided Canaan. It is primarily a book of victory and fulfilled promises. While the Pentateuch covers the events up to the possession of the land, Joshua records the actual entering into the land. The following is a summary of the first six books of the Bible as they relate to the land.

Genesis ----------------------	the promising of the Land
Exodus ----------------------	the leaving for the Land
Leviticus --------------------	the Laws for living in the Land
Numbers --------------------	the wandering outside of the Land (old generation)
Deuteronomy ------------	the preparing for the Land (new generation)
Joshua ---------------------	the possessing of the Land

10. **CHRIST SEEN:**

    Christ is seen as our Joshua (Heb. 4:8), The Captain of our Salvation (Heb. 2:10) wielding the sword of the Spirit, which is the Word of God (Josh. 5:13-15; Eph. 6:12-18), and leading the New Testament Israel into her Inheritance (Heb. 4; Eph. 1:3, 14).

JUDGES

1. **TITLES:**

   A.   Judges = deliverers, saviours (Neh. 9:27)

   B.   The Book of Failure Through Compromise

2. **AUTHOR:**

   Unknown, but usually attributed to Samuel.

3. **DATE:**

   A.   Covers approximately 400 years from the death of Joshua to the death of Samson.

   B.   Possibly written between 1050 and 970 B.C.

4. **KEY WORDS:**

   A.   Judge (d, s) --- 21

   B.   Evil -- 14

   KEY PHRASES:

   A.   "the Spirit of the Lord came upon . . ." -------------------------------- 6

   B.   "no king in Israel; every man did that which
   was right in his own eyes" --- 4

5. **KEY VERSE:** 2:10; 21:25

6. **PURPOSE:**

   A.   To show the spiritual wanderings of Israel in Canaan.

   B.   To show how Israel's compromise led to Israel's failure.

7. **MESSAGE:**

   A.   Because of sin man is always prone to wander from God.

   B.   Departing from God leads to servitude and oppression.

   C.   God manifests His grace by raising up a saviour to bring man back to Himself.

8. **OUTLINE:**

   I.   Compromise In Conquest (Introduction) . . . . Ch. 1:1-2:5
   National Unfaithfulness

   II.   Forsaking The Lord (History) . . . . Ch. 2:6-16:10
   National Servitudes
        A.   Relapses
        B.   Results
        C.   Recoveries

   III.   Anarchy The Final Result (Appendix) . . . . Ch. 17-21
   National Corruption

9. **SUMMARY:**

   This book depicts Israel's settling in the land and the special problems they confronted. It is a book of mixture as we find both victories and defeats, good and evil, revival and apostacy, unity and anarchy. There is a cycle that is repeated seven times in the book that is best summarized in Judges 2:11-19;

   > Departure from the Lord
   > Servitude to enemies
   > Supplication to the Lord
   > Saviour/Judge raised up
   > Return to the Lord

   Though the book covers approximately 400 years of Israel's history, only 111 years were actually spent in servitudes. Though a book of failure, faith is seen in the ministry of the Judges (Heb. 11:32-34).

   NOTE: The book of Judges is not written in strict chronological order, but events are grouped according to spiritual significance.

10. **CHRIST SEEN:**

    Christ is seen as our Judge-Deliverer-Saviour upon whom "the Spirit of the Lord came" bringing deliverance from servitude to sin and Satan.

RUTH

1. **TITLES:**

   A. Ruth = friend, comeliness, beauty
   B. The Book of Grace

2. **AUTHOR:**

   Unknown, but usually attributed to Samuel.

3. **DATE:**

   A. Covers approximately 11 years, "in the days of the judges" (1:1).
   B. Possibly written between 1030 and 970 B.C.

4. **KEY WORDS:**

   A. Kinsman ('s, men) --- 14
   B. Redeem (ing) --- 9
   C. Grace, Favour --- 3
   D. Rest --- 3

5. **KEY VERSE:** 3:13

6. **PURPOSE:**

   A. To extract a positive picture of grace from the period of the judges.
   B. To establish the genealogy of David.
   C. To typify the calling of the Gentiles.

7. **MESSAGE:**

   A. The kinsman redeems by grace into rest, restoring the lost inheritance.
   B. Pure love will overcome all difficulties.

8. **OUTLINE:**

   I. Rest Forsaken . . . . Ch. 1:1-5
   II. Rest Desired . . . . Ch. 1:6-22
   III. Rest Sought . . . . Ch. 2-3
   IV. Rest Secured . . . . Ch. 4

9. **SUMMARY:**

   Two books of the Bible bear the name of a woman; Ruth and Esther. Ruth was a Gentile who married a Jew, and Esther was a Jewess who married a Gentile. The book of Ruth is the only book of the Bible that is wholly devoted to the history of a woman. In chapter one the background is laid. Elimelech, Naomi and their two sons left Bethlehem-Judah because of famine and went to the land of the Moabites (idolatrous descendants of Lot). The two sons married two Moabite girls; Orpah and Ruth. After ten years the father and both sons had died and Naomi decided to return to Bethlehem. Orpah remained behind but Ruth went with her. In chapter two, we are introduced to Boaz the son of Rahab of Jericho (Mt. 1:5). He, being a kinsman of Naomi and Ruth, took notice of Ruth gleaning in his field and treated her kindly. In chapters three and four we see Boaz fulfilling the role of the kinsman-redeemer by buying Elimelech's and his sons' inheritance and by marrying Ruth. The book closes with a genealogy stating the role of Ruth and Boaz in the ancestry of David. This shows that God used Gentile blood to form the chosen family within the chosen nation which would bring forth the Messiah for all nations. Ruth also provides us with a beautiful picture of the church, being a Gentile; a stranger and foreigner to the covenants of promise, who is brought into the commonwealth of Israel by the grace of the kinsman-redeemer (Eph. 2:11-13).

10. **CHRIST SEEN:**

   Christ is seen as a Mighty Man (2:1), the Lord of the Harvest (2:4-17), and our Kinsman-Redeemer, bringing us into union with Himself through grace.

I SAMUEL

1. **TITLES:**

    A. Samuel = asked of God
    B. "The First Book of Kings" -- Septuagint Title

    NOTE: In the Septuagint Version I & II Samuel = I & II Kings; and I & II Kings = III & IV Kings.

    C. The Book of The Monarchy
    D. The Book of The Transition

2. **AUTHOR:**

    Probably written by Samuel, and completed by Nathan and Gad (I Sam. 10:25; I Chr. 29:29).

3. **DATE:**

    A. Covers approximately 115 years from the birth of Samuel to the death of Saul.
    B. Probably written between 1060 and 900 B.C.

4. **KEY WORDS:**

A. Saul ('s) --- 296	D. King ('s) --- 88	G. Anoint (ed) --- 19
B. David ('s) --- 291	E. Priest (s) --- 33	H. Pray (ed, ing) --- 9
C. Samuel --- 131	F. Prophet (s, sy) --- 24	I. Rejected --- 8

5. **KEY VERSE:** 12:23

6. **PURPOSE:**

    A. To establish the united Kingdom of Israel.
    B. To establish the Sceptre of Judah upon David, thus preserving a Godly line unto Messiah.
    C. To give us examples of good and evil character (e.g. Eli, Samuel, Saul and David).

7. **MESSAGE:**

    A. Disobedience will bring the rejection of the anointed (e.g. Eli, the anointed priest, and Saul, the anointed king, were rejected because of disobedience).
    B. A man of God will be a man of prayer, constantly interceding for the needs of the people.

8. **OUTLINE:**

    I.   Samuel: From Theocracy to Monarchy . . . . Ch. 1-7
    II. Saul: From Election to Rejection . . . . Ch. 8-15
    III. David: From Anointing to Humiliation . . . . Ch. 16-31

9. **SUMMARY:**

    The book is simply divided into three sections in relation to the three main characters (Samuel, Saul, and David). It is a book of biographies. Samuel is the most important figure in this period of Israel's history. He is a priest, the last of the judges, the first of the prophets, and anoints the first king. Thus Israel's form of government has moved from theocracy (Exodus to Joshua) into periods of anarchy (Judges), and now in I Samuel moves into monarchy.

    NOTE: Samuel is known as "the Prophet of Prayer" (I Sam. 12:23; Jer. 15:1).

10. **CHRIST SEEN:**

    Christ is seen as our Anointed Prophet, Priest, King and Intercessor. He is seen as the only true claimant to the Sceptre of Judah, the Throne of David and the Everlasting Kingdom of Israel (Lk. 1:31-33).

II SAMUEL

1. **TITLES:**

   A. Samuel = asked of God
   B. "The Second Book of Kings" -- Septuagint Title
   C. The Book of The Monarchy
   D. The Book of The King

2. **AUTHOR:**

   Possibly written by Nathan and Gad (I Chr. 29:29).

3. **DATE:**

   A. Covers approximately 40 years, from David's enthronement to just before his death.
   B. Probably written between 970 and 900 B.C.

4. **KEY WORDS:**

   A. King ('s, dom) --- 290
   B. David ('s) --- 286

   KEY PHRASES:

   A. "before the Lord" -- 10
   B. "enquired of the Lord" -- 4

5. **KEY VERSE:** 5:12

6. **PURPOSE:**

   A. To establish the Davidic Covenant, Seed, Throne and Kingdom (II Sam. 7; Ps. 89).
   B. To record the reign of David including both his triumphs and his trials.

7. **MESSAGE:**

   A. Patience and dependence upon God are necessary for the fulfillment of His promises. (Shown by David's preparation to be king from humiliation (I Sam.) to exaltation (II Sam.).)
   B. Obedience will bring blessing for those in Covenant relationship with God. (Shown by the first 20 years of David's reign.)
   C. Sometimes pardoned sin is still punished. (Shown by the last 20 years of David's reign.)

8. **OUTLINE:**

   I. David's Triumphs: 20 years of Blessing . . . . Ch. 1-10
      A. David: King Over Judah (7 years) . . . . Ch. 1-4
      B. David: King Over All Israel (33 years) . . . . Ch. 5-10
   II. David's Trials: 20 years of Judgment . . . . Ch. 11-24
      A. David's Downfall: Pardon and Punishment . . . . Ch. 11-21
      B. Closing Scenes . . . . Ch. 22-24

9. **SUMMARY:**

   This book is basically a biography of David setting him forth as the anointed political and religious king. David was "a man after God's own heart" (I Sam. 13:14), and thus he established the Tabernacle of David and the order of worship set forth in the Psalms (II Sam. 23:1, 2). He obeyed the Covenant and was constantly "enquiring before the Lord". However, this is the only book that also records David's downfall and the tragic consequences.

10. **CHRIST SEEN:**

   Christ, "the Son of David", is seen as the "Greater King David" who establishes the New Testament order of worship. The Davidic Covenant is the covenant of Messiah as the ultimate political (king) and religious (priest) ruler of the world.

I KINGS

1. **TITLES:**

   A. "The Third Book of the Kings" -- Septuagint Title
   B. The Book of The Monarchy
   C. The Book of The Disruption

2. **AUTHOR:**

   Ascribed by tradition (the Talmud) to Jeremiah, who possibly incorporated records made by Nathan and Gad (I Chr. 29:29).

3. **DATE:**

   A. Covers approximately 120 years, from the death of David to the death of Jehoshaphat.
   B. Probably written between 600 and 580 B.C.

4. **KEY WORDS:**

   A. King ('s, s) -- 310
   B. House -- 173
   C. Prophet (s) --- 50

   KEY PHRASES:

   A. "Word of the Lord" -------------------------------------- 33
   B. "as his father David" ----------------------------------- 9
   C. "the sins (or way) of Jeroboam" ----------------------- 8

5. **KEY VERSES:** 22:10, 19

6. **PURPOSE:**

   A. To give the history of the establishment and glory of the united kingdom.
   B. To give the history of the disruption of the kingdom into two houses, two kingdoms and two dynasties with their declines.

7. **MESSAGE:**

   A. God's Throne is above all earthly thrones.
   B. Kings succeed or fail according to their relationship to the heavenly throne and their response to the Word of the Lord through the ministry of the prophets.

8. **OUTLINE:**

   I. The Kingdom United . . . . Ch. 1-11   One House-One King
      A. The Establishment of the Kingdom . . . . Ch. 1-2
      B. The Glory of the Kingdom . . . . Ch. 3-11
   II. The Kingdom Divided . . . . Ch. 12-22   Two Houses-Two Kings
      A. The Disruption of the Kingdom . . . . Ch. 12
      B. The Decline of the Kingdom . . . . Ch. 13-22

9. **SUMMARY:**

   The book of I Kings covers the glorious reign of Solomon, the dividing of the kingdom after his death, and the history of the divided kingdom through the reigns of Ahab in the north (Israel) and Jehoshaphat in the south (Judah). All the kings of Israel and Judah lined up under two "standard men", David the godly king and Jeroboam the ungodly king.

10. **CHRIST SEEN:**

   Christ is seen as the King of Peace and Glory, the Wisdom of God (I Cor. 1:30), the builder of God's Temple (Eph. 2:20-22), the "Greater Than Solomon" (Mt. 12:42) and The Prophet of God -- the Word made flesh (Jn. 1:14). His Throne is above all thrones: King of Kings and Lord of Lords. (Rev. 19:16).

II KINGS

1. **TITLES:**

   A. "The Fourth Book of the Kings" -- Septuagint Title
   B. The Book of the Collapse of the Monarchy
   C. The Book of The Dispersion

2. **AUTHOR:**

   Ascribed by tradition (The Talmud) to Jeremiah.

3. **DATE:**

   A. Covers a period of about 300 years, from King Jehoshaphat of Judah and King Ahaziah of Israel through to the Assyrian and Babylonian Captivities.
   B. Probably written between 600 and 580 B.C.

4. **KEY WORDS:**

   A. King ('s, s) --- 382
   B. House --- 134
   C. Prophet (s) -- 33

   KEY PHRASES:

   A. "man of God" -- 36
   B. "the Word of the Lord" --- 16
   C. "did that which was evil in the sight of the Lord" ------------- 20
   D. "did that which was right in the sight of the Lord" ----------- 6

5. **KEY VERSES:** 17:13, 14

6. **PURPOSE:**

   A. To give the contemporary histories of the Kingdom of Israel and the Kingdom of Judah through to their respective captivities (Israel -- Assyrian Captivity, Judah -- Babylonian Captivity).

7. **MESSAGE:**

   A. Rejecting the Word of the Lord through His prophets and lapsing into idolatry and apostacy, will result in rejection and captivity (II K. 17:13-23).
   B. Man is unable to successfully rule himself.

8. **OUTLINE:**

   I. The Annals of Israel (Northern Kingdom) . . . . Ch. 1-10
   Ending with the death of Jehu, Israel's tenth king
   II. The Annals of Israel and Judah (Alternating) . . . . Ch. 11-17
   Ending with the Assyrian Captivity of Israel
   III. The Annals of Judah (Southern Kingdom) . . . . Ch. 18-25
   Ending with the Babylonian Captivity of Judah

9. **SUMMARY:**

   In the Hebrew Scriptures I and II Kings formed one book. Viewed as such this one book covers Israel's history as follows: It opens with King Solomon, the first successor to the throne of David, and the Temple being built. It closes with King Zedekiah, the last successor to the throne of David, being slain and the temple destroyed. It takes us from the death of King David of Jerusalem to the death of King Nebuchadnezzar of Babylon. II Kings itself begins where I Kings leaves off and continues the record of the two Kingdoms of Israel and Judah through to Israel's captivity to Assyria and Judah's Captivity to Babylon over one hundred years later.

10. **CHRIST SEEN:**

   Christ is seen as the Righteous King, the Man of God and the Word of the Lord personified (II K. 3:12; Jn. 1:14).

I CHRONICLES

1. **TITLES:**
   - A. Chronicles = "The Words of the Days" -- Hebrew Title
   - B. "Supplements" -- Septuagint Title
   - C. "Things Omitted" -- Greek Translators' Title
   - D. The Book of The Theocracy

2. **AUTHOR:**

   Probably written by Ezra.

3. **DATE:**
   - A. Covers about 40 years, from the death of Saul to the beginning of Solomon's reign.
   - B. Probably written about 450 B.C.

4. **KEY WORDS:**
   - A. David ('s) --- 189
   - B. House -- 106
   - C. Begat -- 86
   - D. King ('s, s) -- 76

5. **KEY VERSES:**
   - A. 29:26 ------ "David reigned over all Israel"
   - B. 29:12 ------ "Thou reignest over all"

6. **PURPOSE:**
   - A. To give the genealogies leading up to the kingly throne of David and the priestly ministrations.
   - B. To give a history of King David's reign.
   - C. To record the order of worship established in David's Tabernacle, and the preparations for the building of the Temple under Solomon.

7. **MESSAGE:**
   - A. God is Sovereign.
   - B. Man derives his authority from God by submitting to God's authority.

8. **OUTLINE:**
   - I. Genealogies . . . . Ch. 1-9
     - A. Patriarchal . . . . Ch. 1-2
     - B. Royal . . . . Ch. 3-5
     - C. Priestly . . . . Ch. 6-9
   - II. History of the Theocracy . . . . Ch. 10-21
     - A. Saul's Death . . . . Ch. 10
     - B. David's Reign . . . . Ch. 11-21
   - III. The Temple . . . . Ch. 22-29
     - A. Revelation and Preparation . . . . Ch. 22-27
     - B. David's Charge to Solomon and Death . . . . Ch. 28-29

9. **SUMMARY:**

   King David is the central figure in this book just as he is in II Samuel. He is seen establishing the order of worship in the Tabernacle of David, receiving the revelation of the Temple, preparing for its building and turning the work over to Solomon.

10. **CHRIST SEEN:**

    Christ is seen as the "Greater King David" who receives the revelation and makes preparation before his death for the building of the spiritual Temple (The Church -- Eph. 2:20, 21), under the ministry of the Holy Spirit (Solomon).

II CHRONICLES

1. **TITLES:**

    A. Chronicles = "The Words of the Days" -- Hebrew Title
    B. "Supplements" -- Septuagint Title
    C. "Things Omitted" -- Greek Translators' Title
    D. The Book of Relapse and Reformation

2. **AUTHOR:**

    Probably written by Ezra.

3. **DATE:**

    A. Covers about 400 years, from the beginning of Solomon's reign to the decree of Cyrus for the rebuilding of Jerusalem.
    B. Probably written about 450 B.C.

4. **KEY WORDS:**

    A. King ('s, s) --- 289
    B. House (Most referring to the Temple) --------------------------- 203
    C. Jerusalem -- 127
    D. Priest ('s, s) --- 90
    E. Prophet (s) --- 26

    KEY PHRASE:

    A. "Seek the Lord" -- 13

5. **KEY VERSES:** 7:14; 15:2-4

6. **PURPOSE:**

    A. To give the history of the Kings of Judah from Solomon, builder of the temple, through to the destruction of the temple under Zedekiah, the last king of Judah, and the Babylonian Captivity.
    B. To show the relationship of the enthroned Kings to the Temple. (Temple vs. Throne)

7. **MESSAGE:**

    A. God will be found of those that seek and serve Him but He will forsake those who forsake Him.
    B. Spiritual victory is determined by whether or not one has "prepared his heart to seek the Lord" (11:16, 12:14, 19:3, and 30:19).

8. **OUTLINE:**

    I. The Reign of Solomon . . . . Ch. 1-9
       A. Solomon's Kingdom . . . . Ch. 1, 8, 9
       B. Solomon's Temple . . . . Ch. 2-7
    II. The Kings of Judah . . . . Ch. 10-36
       A. Relapses . . . . Ch. 10-13, 21-23, 25-28, 33, 36
       B. Reformations . . . . Ch. 14-20, 24, 29-32, 34, 35

9. **SUMMARY:**

    A. Three Viewpoints of the Kingdom Period:

       1. The books of I & II Kings are written from a royal point of view emphasizing the throne.
       2. The books of I & II Chronicles are written from a priestly point of view emphasizing the temple.
       3. The books of the Prophets are written from a prophetic point of view emphasizing the Divine relationship between throne and temple.

    B. The book of II Chronicles is similar to the book of Judges in that it shows periods of relapses and periods of reformation.

10. **CHRIST SEEN:**

    Christ is seen as our Prophet, Priest and King; the Cleanser of the Temple who brings periods of Reformation after periods of Relapse (Heb. 9:10, 11).

EZRA

1. **TITLES:**

   A. Ezra = help, helper
   B. The Book of the Remnant
   C. The Book of Restoration

2. **AUTHOR:**

   Written by Ezra. The books of Ezra and Nehemiah were one book until the 3rd Century B.C., indicating that Ezra and Nehemiah possibly wrote in collaboration.

3. **DATE:**

   A. Covers a period of about 80 years, from the decree of Cyrus to a time shortly after Ezra's arrival at Jerusalem.
   B. Probably written between 440 and 400 B.C.

4. **KEY WORDS:**

   A. Jerusalem --- 48
   B. Law (8), Commandment (2), Word (1) -------------------------------- 11

   KEY PHRASE:

   A. "go up", "went up" --- 11

5. **KEY VERSES:** 2:1, 6:14

6. **PURPOSE:**

   A. To show the return of the remnants under Zerubbabel and Ezra from the Babylonian Captivity, the rebuilding of the Temple and the restoration of Jerusalem.
   B. To show the fulfillment of the Word of the Lord through Jeremiah and Isaiah concerning the fall of Babylon and the restoration of Judah to Jerusalem. (Jer. 25:8-14; Is. 44:26-45:1).

7. **MESSAGE:**

   A. God stirs up heathen nations for His sovereign purposes (Divine Sovereignty).
   B. God's purposes can be fulfilled through human vessels (Human Responsibility).

8. **OUTLINE:**

   I. Return of the First Remnant under Zerubbabel ...... Ch. 1-6
   (Lapse of about 63 years between Ch. 6 & 7).
   II. Return of the Second Remnant under Ezra .... Ch. 7-10

9. **SUMMARY:**

   In the book of Ezra, we see Zerubbabel bringing back a remnant of about 50,000 Jews with certain of the sacred vessels for the temple, and the beginning of the rebuilding of the temple. Then we see Ezra, the priestly scribe, bringing back a second remnant of about 2,000 Jews with further of the sacred vessels for the temple, and the religious, social, and civil reformation that followed.

   NOTE: The restoration of Judah to the land and the rebuilding of the temple was not only a fulfillment of the prophetic word, but was designed to hold the Jews in the land until the birth of Messiah according to Daniel's prophecy (Dan. 9:24-27).

10. **CHRIST SEEN:**

    Christ is seen as our Governor (Zerubbabel) and our Priest, Scribe and Restorer (Ezra) of Religious, Social and Civil Order.

NEHEMIAH

1. **TITLES:**

    A. Nehemiah = consolation or Jehovah is comfort
    B. The Book of Restoration
    C. The Book of Reconstruction

2. **AUTHOR:**

    Written by Nehemiah. It is mainly his autobiography.

3. **DATE:**

    A. Covers a period of about 16 years, beginning about 12 years after the close of Ezra.
    B. Probably written between 440 and 400 B.C. It was the last Old Testament historical book to be written.

4. **KEY WORDS:**

    A. Gate (s) --- 41
    B. Wall (s) --- 36
    C. Repaired -- 35
    D. Build (ed, ers, est, t) --- 24
    E. Work (s) -- 23
    F. Pray (ed, er) --- 8

5. **KEY VERSES:** 4:6, 9

6. **PURPOSE:**

    A. To show how that under Nehemiah, the walls and 12 gates of Jerusalem were repaired and rebuilt, and the people were revived.
    B. To give to the church principles of restoration.

7. **MESSAGE:**

    A. God's purpose is to restore that which has been lost and to reconstruct that which has been broken down.
    B. The conditions for successful work for God are prayer, pain, and perserverance.

8. **OUTLINE:**

    I.   Rebuilding of the Walls . . . . Ch. 1-7
    II.   Revival of Religion . . . . Ch. 8-12
    III. Reformation of the People . . . . Ch. 13

9. **SUMMARY:**

    Nehemiah sets before us an example of Godly character and leadership. At the call of God he renounced his life of luxury and high position in the palace of Shushan for a life of toil, danger, hardship, and opposition from false brethren within and enemies without in the work of restoration. He was a man of faith, wisdom, courage, and perserverance; a man of prayer and energy, able to inspire others to work as well as work himself.

    NOTE: Ezra and Nehemiah together show the fulfillment of certain areas of the notable "Seventy Week Prophecy" given to Daniel in Babylon. "From the going forth of the commandment to restore and to build Jerusalem (Ezra) . . . the street shall be built again and the wall, even in troublous times." (Nehemiah) (Dan. 9:25).

10. **CHRIST SEEN:**

    Christ is seen as the Governor of Judah (Mt. 2:6) who left heaven's palaces (Ps. 45:8), and is revealed as the Man of Prayer and Work (Jn. 17 Mt. 16:18) in the Spiritual Restoration of Jerusalem.

ESTHER

1. **TITLES:**

   A. Esther = star, secret, hidden
   B. The Book of <u>Providence</u>

2. **AUTHOR:**

   Possibly written by <u>Mordecai</u> (9:20).

3. **DATE:**

   A. Covers approximately 10 years, from the third year (1:3) of the reign of Ahasuerus to the twelfth year (3:7) of his reign. Chronologically it occurs between the sixth and seventh chapters of Ezra.
   B. Probably written between 450 and 420 B.C.

4. **KEY WORDS:**

   A. King ('s) --- 195
   B. Jew (s, s') -- 53
   C. Queen --- 27

5. **KEY VERSE:** 4:14

6. **PURPOSE:**

   A. To illustrate God's <u>providential</u> care for the Jews that did not return with the first remnant.
   B. To recount the origin of the Jewish feast of Purim (3:6, 7; 9:26-28).

7. **MESSAGE:**

   A. Though unseen, the hand of Divine <u>providence</u> guides, guards, and over-rules in, through and above the affairs of men, keeping watch and preserving His own elect.
   B. Those who attempt to destroy the people of God will be destroyed themselves.

8. **OUTLINE:**

   I. The Feast of <u>Ahasuerus</u> .... Ch. 1-2
   II. The Feast of <u>Esther</u> .... Ch. 3-7
   III. The Feast of <u>Purim</u> .... Ch. 8-10

9. **SUMMARY:**

   In this book we see King Ahasuerus of Persia setting aside Queen Vashti (<u>Feast of Ahasuerus</u>). Esther, who was then chosen to be the bride-queen, was brought in and prepared by the ministries of Mordecai and Hegai (<u>Feast of Esther</u>). Then when Haman, the Agagite, rose up against the Jews, Esther called a national fast and at the risk of her own life brought deliverance to the Jewish people. <u>The Feast of Purim</u> was then initiated to be celebrated annually to commemorate the death of Haman (hung on the gallows he had prepared for Mordecai) and the deliverance and preservation of the Jews. Esther is the last of three post-exilic historical books;

Ezra -------- Restoration of the <u>Temple</u> -------------------------------	Religious
Nehemiah-- Reconstruction of the <u>City Walls</u> -------------------------	Political
Esther ------ Preservation of the <u>House of Judah</u> ----------------------	National

   NOTE: The name of God is not mentioned once in Esther but is hidden in Hebrew acrostic form four times in the book.

10. **CHRIST SEEN:**

   Christ is seen as the <u>King</u>, for whom the church (Esther) is prepared to be married to by the ministry of the Word (Mordecai) and the Spirit (Hegai).

JOB

1. **TITLES:**

    A. Job = persecuted; he that weeps, speaks, or cries out of a hollow place; sorrowful; the one who turns to God
    B. The Book of the Mystery of Suffering
    C. The Book of Blessing Through Suffering

2. **AUTHOR:**

    Probably written by Job himself (19:23, 24) since he lived 140 years after these events took place (42:16). Some have suggested Moses or Elihu as possible authors.

3. **DATE:**

    A. Covers a period of only a few weeks or possibly a few months time.
    B. Probably written during the time of the patriarchs. It is considered by most to be the first book of the Bible written.

4. **KEY WORDS:**

    A. Wicked (ly, ness) --- 48
    B. Right (eous, eousness) -- 32
    C. Why --- 16
    D. Afflict (ed, tion) --- 11

    KEY PHRASE:

    A. "answered and said" -- 27

5. **KEY VERSES:**   1:9 (Satan); 2:3 (God); 13:15 (Job); 42:5

6. **PURPOSE:**

    A. To deal with the problem as to how the suffering of the godly can be reconciled with the justice and love of God.
    B. To set forth Job as God's example of patience under suffering (James 5:11).

7. **MESSAGE:**

    A. The cause and purpose of the affliction of the righteous often remain a mystery to the sufferer.
    B. God uses affliction to reveal character and to expose areas of weakness that need to come under His dealings.
    C. God is sovereign and Satan can do only what God allows.

8. **OUTLINE:**

    I. Prologue . . . . Ch. 1-2
        A. Scenes on Earth (1:1-5, 13-22; 2:7-13)
        B. Scenes in Heaven (1:6-12; 2:1-6)
    II. Dialogue . . . . Ch. 3-41
        A. Three Triads of Discourses . . . . Ch. 4-37
        B. God's Closing Intervention . . . . Ch. 38-41
    III. Epilogue . . . . Ch. 42

9. **SUMMARY:**

    Job, a godly man, suffered the loss of his fortune, family, and personal health. He was baffled by his affliction not knowing that he was the target of a conflict between God and Satan. His three friends; Eliphaz, Bildad, and Zophar, "comforted" him by trying to convince him that his suffering was punishment from God because of his personal sin. Elihu, having partial light on the situation, explained Job's suffering as being chastisement sent to purify Job. Finally, God spoke putting Job and the others in their place. Job's suffering was designed, first of all, as a trial in which Job could prove himself in opposition to Satan, but since Job did not pass through the trial entirely without blemish, it also had the effect of purifying him. In the end, Job was blessed with a double portion of all he had before.

    NOTE: There are rich Messianic prophecies in Job (9:32, 33, 19:25-27).

    NOTE: Many principles of counselling can be gleaned from this book.

10. **CHRIST SEEN:**

    Christ is seen as the Priest, whose patient suffering was inflicted by Satan but purposed by God.

PSALMS

1. **TITLES:**
   A. Psalm = a song of praise (accompanied by an instrument)
   B. "Songs of Praise" -- Hebrew Title
   C. "The Psalter" -- Greek Title
   D. The Book of Prayer and Praise

2. **AUTHORS:**
   The Known Authors Are:

   A. Psalms of David ------------------------------- 73
   B. Psalms of Asaph ------------------------------- 12
   C. Psalms of the Sons of Korah --------------- 10
   D. Psalms of/for Solomon ---------------------- 2
   E. Psalm of Moses ------------------------------- 1
   F. Psalm of Heman ------------------------------- 1
   G. Psalm of Ethan -------------------------------- 1

3. **DATE:**
   Due to the variety of authors the time period ranges from Moses through to Ezra.

4. **KEY WORDS:**
   A. Praise (s, d, ing) ------------------------------- 189
   B. Heart ('s, s, s') --------------------------------- 132
   C. Righteous (ness, ly) --------------------------- 132
   D. Sing, Song --------------------------------------- 122
   E. Wicked (ness, ly) ------------------------------- 109
   F. Bless (ed, ing) ----------------------------------- 102
   G. Evil, Good --- 102
   H. Sin, Iniquity ------------------------------------- 98
   I. Pray (er) --- 39

5. **KEY VERSES:** 150:1-6

6. **PURPOSE:**
   A. To preserve in poetic form the fundamental doctrines of God and man, and their relationship in creation and redemption.
   B. To show the blessed state of the righteous in their praise and worship of God and the judgment of the unrighteous who reject God.
   C. To present the proper attitudes and methods of the worship of God that is in spirit and truth.

7. **MESSAGE:**
   A. Only the righteous and the good who have forsaken sin and iniquity are blessed and can offer praise and worship to the Lord from their hearts.

8. **OUTLINE:**
   Ancient Hebrew Saying: "Moses gave to Israel the five Books of the Law and corresponding with these, David gave Israel the five Books of Psalms."

   I. The Genesis Book concerning Man . . . . Ps. 1-41
   II. The Exodus Book concerning Israel . . . . Ps. 42-72
   III. The Leviticus Book concerning the Sanctuary . . . . Ps. 73-89
   IV. The Numbers Book concerning the Earth and the Nations . Ps. 90-106
   V. The Deuteronomy Book concerning the Word of God . . . Ps. 107-150

9. **SUMMARY:**
   The Psalms are a "complete Bible" in themselves. Possibly every subject that pertains to God and Man in Creation and Redemption's plan is referred to in its great themes. Most of the Psalms can be grouped into one of the following categories; Messianic, Penitential, Imprecatory, Acrostic, Hallelujah, Songs of Degrees, Historical, Devotional, Worship, and Didactic. There is a Psalm for every occasion, suitable for every feeling, longing, desire, emotion, and expression in the heart and life of man. The book of Psalms is the very heart of the Bible.

   NOTE: The Messianic Psalms portray the whole life story of Christ from His pre-existence to His eternal throne.

10. **CHRIST SEEN:**

   Christ is seen as the "Beloved" of God singing praise in the midst of the Church (Heb. 2:12).

PROVERBS

1. **TITLES:**
   A. Proverb = comparison
   B. The Book of Instruction
   C. The Book of Wisdom

2. **AUTHOR:**
   Written and collected by Solomon with the possible exception of the last two chapters. (I Kings 4:32; Eccl. 12:9).

3. **DATE:**
   Written mostly by Solomon (about 950 B.C.), but not completed until the time of Hezekiah (about 715 B.C.; see 25:1).

4. **KEY WORDS:**

A.	Wise (ly, r), Wisdom	124	E.	Knowledge	42
B.	Fool (s, ish), Folly	97	F.	Instruction (ed)	27
C.	Heart (s)	85	G.	Judgment	18
D.	Understand (ing, eth)	66			

   KEY PHRASE:
   A. "fear of the Lord" --------------------------- 16

5. **KEY VERSES:** 1:7, 9:10

6. **PURPOSE:**
   A. The purpose of the book is plainly stated in Ch. 1:2-6.
   B. To show the application of divine wisdom to the various aspects of the daily life in this evil world.
   C. To define and contrast wisdom and foolishness.

7. **MESSAGE:**
   A. Godliness is intensely practical.
   B. The end results of wisdom are vastly superior to the evil end of folly.

8. **OUTLINE:**

   I. Introduction -- The Purpose .... Ch. 1:1-7
   II. Words of Wisdom For "My Son" .... Ch. 1:8-9:18
       A Collection of 15 Didactic Poems
   III. Proverbs of Solomon .... Ch. 10-22:16
       A Collection of 375 Single-Verse Proverbs
       A. Contrastive Proverbs .... Ch. 10-15
       B. Completive and Comparative Proverbs .... Ch. 16-22:16
   IV. Words of The Wise .... Ch. 22:17-24:34
       A Collection of 35 Proverbs & Short Poems
   V. Proverbs Collected by Hezekiah....................... Ch. 25-29
       A Collection of 127 Proverbs
   VI. The Words of Agur .... Ch. 30
   VII. The Words of Lemuel .... Ch. 31:1-9
   VII. The Virtuous Woman Acrostic .... Ch. 31:10-31

9. **SUMMARY:**
   It has been said that "What the Psalms are to the devotional life, the Proverbs are to the practical life." This book contains no prophecy and little doctrine, but instead is an instructional book, applying the divine wisdom to daily life. It warns against such things as bad company, impurity, intemperance, quarreling, lying, trickery in business, and taking of bribes. It condemns idleness, slothfulness, pride, and avarice. It commends liberality to those in need. It teaches the fear of the Lord, obedience of children to parents, duty of parents to properly train their children, and the woman's role in the home. It also contains special instruction for the young man just going out into the world.

10. **CHRIST SEEN:**
    Christ is seen as "the Wisdom of God" (I Cor. 1:24, 30), "in whom are hid all the treasures of wisdom and knowledge" (Col. 2:3). Note especially the sections where wisdom is personified and speaks (1:20-33; 8:1-36).

ECCLESIASTES

1. **TITLES:**

    A.   Ecclesiastes = the preacher
    B.   The Book of Vanity
    C.   The Book of Human Wisdom

2. **AUTHOR:**

    Written by The Preacher who many have understood to be a reference to Solomon.

3. **DATE:**

    Possibly written about 935 B.C. during Solomon's old age.

4. **KEY WORDS:**

    A.   Wise (ly), Wisdom --- 54
    B.   Heart -- 40
    C.   Vanity (ies) -- 37
    D.   Fool (s, ish), Folly -- 32

    KEY PHRASES:

    A.   "under the sun (heaven)" --------------------------------------- 31
    B.   "vexation of spirit" -- 10

5. **KEY VERSES:**   1:13-14; 12:13-14

6. **PURPOSE:**

    A.   To solicit trust in God by discounting trust in any other.
    B.   To disillusion those who would put their trust in the things of this world by pointing out the vanity of all earthly things.
    C.   To comfort the godly, showing them how to face the difficulties of life.

7. **MESSAGE:**

    A.   Apart from God, life is full of weariness and disappointment.
    B.   Men who know the vanity of all things are well prepared for the trials of depressing times.
    C.   The whole duty of man is to fear God, and keep His commandments (Ch. 12:13).

8. **OUTLINE:**

    I.   Introduction .... Ch. 1:1-11
    II.   The Vanity of All Things .... Ch. 1:12-6:12
    III.   Counsel Concerning Wisdom .... Ch. 7:1-12:7
    IV.   Conclusion .... Ch. 12:8-14

9. **SUMMARY:**

    King Solomon, being in a position to satisfy his every desire, attempted to do so materially, sensually, emotionally, and intellectually. He soon discovered that life without the fear of God was empty and futile. Whether Solomon wrote this book or someone else authored it using his experiences, the message comes through loud and clear that the whole duty of man is to fear God and keep His commandments (12:13). "The Preacher" constructed his sermon very wisely first pointing out the vanity of all things "under the sun" (in the earthly realm) and showing the folly of human wisdom apart from the Divine Wisdom. Then he leads us to the conclusion that only God can bring fulfillment and thus our hope and trust must be in Him alone.

    NOTE: Relate Jas. 2:13, 17, 18 to Proverbs and Jas. 2:14-16 to Ecclesiastes.

10. **CHRIST SEEN:**

    Christ is seen as The Preacher, the Son of David, the Wisdom of God, and the King of the Jerusalem "from above" (Eccl. 1:1; I Cor. 1:24; Gal. 4:26).

SONG OF SOLOMON

1. **TITLES:**

   A. Canticles -- Latin Title
   B. The Song of Songs -- (1:1 with I Kings 4:32)
   C. The Book of Love

2. **AUTHOR:**

   Written by Solomon (1:1).

3. **DATE:**

   Written about 970 B.C.

4. **KEY WORDS:**

   A. Beloved ('s) --- 33
   B. Love (th, s, ly) --- 33
   C. Fair (est) --- 14

   KEY PHRASE:

   A. "daughters of Jerusalem" ------------------------------------- 7

5. **KEY VERSES:**

   The Three Stages of Love --

   A. 2:16 "My beloved is mine, and I am his"
   B. 6:3 "I am my beloved's and my beloved is mine"
   C. 7:10 "I am my beloved's, and his desire is toward me"

6. **PURPOSE:**

   A. Literal: To glorify marriage and wedded love.
   B. Mystical: To represent the love of Jehovah for Israel. (Hos. 2:19, 20 Recognized by Jewish students from early times)
   C. Prophetical: To represent the love of Christ and the Church. (II Cor. 11:2, Eph. 5:22-33; Rev. 19:7-9)
   D. Devotional: To represent the love of Christ and the Believer.

7. **MESSAGE:**

   A. Our relationship to Christ is to be a growing love relationship.
   B. True love is strong and unquenchable (Ch. 8:7).

8. **OUTLINE:**

I.	First Song ----------	Initial Love	Ch. 1:1-2:7
II.	Second Song -------	Faltering Love	Ch. 2:8-3:5
III.	Third Song ---------	Growing Love.............	Ch. 3:6-5:1
IV.	Fourth Song ------	Transforming Love	Ch. 5:2-8:5
V.	Fifth Song ---------	Mature Love..............	Ch. 8:5-14

9. **SUMMARY:**

   Solomon composed over a thousand songs (I K. 4:32) and of all his songs this, the Song of Songs, was the most excellent. It is actually made up of five songs which together show the progressive development of the love relationship between a bride and bridegroom. It also describes the many obstacles that the bride has to overcome in order to be truly united with her beloved. The two main characters that speak in this song are the bridegroom, who speaks of his bride as his "love", and the bride, who refers to her bridegroom as her "beloved". There is a chorus of the daughters of Jerusalem that are heard throughout the song as well as a group of observors that are heard from in chapter three.

10. **CHRIST SEEN:**

    Christ is seen as the King of Peace (Solomon) and the Beloved Bridegroom Lover of the Church, who is "the fair one and undefiled", (Shulamite means "peaceable", "perfect") "This is a great mystery; but I speak concerning Christ and the church." (Eph. 5:32)

ISAIAH

1. **TITLES:**
   A. Isaiah = salvation of Jehovah or Jah is helper
   B. The Book of "the Gospel According to Isaiah"
   C. The Book of Salvation

2. **AUTHOR:**
   Written by Isaiah, the prophet of Redemption, who prophesied concerning the House of Israel, but ministered mainly to the House of Judah.

3. **DATE:**
   A. Isaiah's ministry covered a period of about 50 years (740 - 690 B.C.) beginning in the later years of Uzziah's reign, continuing through the reigns of Jotham and Ahaz, and ending in Hezekiah's reign (Is. 1:1).
   B. Written between 740 and 690 B.C.

4. **KEY WORDS:**
   A. Righteous (ly, ness) -- 64
   B. Save (d), Salvation, Saviour ---------------------------- 55
   C. Judge (s, ing, ment) ---------------------------------- 52
   D. Deliver (ed, eth, ance) -------------------------------- 32
   E. Comfort (ed, eth, edst, s, ably) ---------------------- 18

   KEY PHRASE:
   A. "Holy One (of Israel)" ---------------------------------- 30

5. **KEY VERSES:** 12:6; 56:1; 61:1-3

6. **PURPOSE:**
   A. To show that even though Judah had a "form of godliness", it was corrupt morally, religiously, and politically.
   B. To predict the destiny of the Gentile nations.
   C. To give a panoramic prophetic picture of the life and ministry of the Messiah.

7. **MESSAGE:**
   A. Through judgment the Holy One of Israel brings salvation, righteousness, and comfort.
   B. Only through the Messiah will salvation come to all the nations.

8. **OUTLINE:**
   I. Book of Judgment (Prophetic) .... Ch. 1-35
   (Judah, Israel, and the Gentiles)
   Judgments (1-12), Burdens (13-27), Woes (28-35)
   II. Book of Deliverance (Historic) .... Ch. 36-39
   (Assyria, Judah, and Hezekiah)
   III. Book of Comfort (Messianic) .... Ch. 40-66
   (Jehovah, Messiah, and the Kingdom)

9. **SUMMARY:**
   Isaiah's prophecies are not only applicable in judgment to the destinies of Judah, Israel, and the Gentiles but also to the blessing of all nations through the Messiah and the Church. Isaiah gives the most comprehensive life-story of Messiah, "the salvation of Jehovah", of all the prophetical books combined. He refers more to the Messiah, His Kingdom, and the coming in of the Gentiles than all the other prophets combined.
   NOTE: There are more quotations from Isaiah in the New Testament than any other prophetical book (over 60).

10. **CHRIST SEEN:**
   Christ is seen in His Messianic Glory as the Holy One of Israel (Mk. 1:24) our Salvation (Mt. 1:21), our Righteousness (I Cor. 1:30), and Comfort (Jn. 14:16, 18). All Judgment has been committed to Him (Jn. 5:22).

JEREMIAH

1. **TITLES:**

    A. Jeremiah = exalted of Jehovah, or appointed of Jehovah
    B. The Book To The Backslider

2. **AUTHOR:**

    Written by Jeremiah, the prophet of Judgment, who prophesied to the House of Judah. He also wrote Lamentations.

3. **DATE:**

    A. Jeremiah's ministry covered a period of about 66 years (626 - 560 B.C.), beginning in the reign of Josiah, continuing through the reigns of Jehoahaz, Jehoiakim, Jeconiah, and ending after the reign of Zedekiah, Judah's last king.
    B. Written between 620 and 560 B.C.

4. **KEY WORDS:**

A.	Judah	181	G.	Heart (s)	62
B.	Babylon	160	H.	Sin (s, ned), Iniquity (ies)	52
C.	Jerusalem	108	I.	Judge (d, st, ment)	27
D.	Evil (s)	100	J.	Forsake (n)	24
E.	Return (ed), Turn (ed)	95	K.	Backsliding (s)	13
F.	Captive (s, ity)	64			

    KEY PHRASES:

    A. "the Word of the Lord (came)" ———————————— 70
    B. "the Lord of hosts, the God of Israel" ———————— 35
    C. "carried away" ———————————————————— 25

5. **KEY VERSES:** 2:19; 3:22; 13:19

6. **PURPOSE:**

    A. Historically: To give the history of the last five kings of the House of Judah, the destruction of the temple, desolation of the city, and the captivity of the nation to Babylon.
    B. Spiritually: To show God's grace and mercy in calling a backslidden nation to return to the Lord.
    C. Prophetically: To predict the destiny of the chosen nation and the Gentile nations.

7. **MESSAGE:**

    A. The Word of the Lord calls backsliders to forsake their iniquity and return to the Lord.
    B. All evil is certain to be judged by captivity.
    C. After calling them to repentance, God will forsake those who forsake Him.

8. **OUTLINE:**

    I.   Jeremiah's Call and Commission . . . . Ch. 1
    II. Prophecies Before the Captivity . . . . Ch. 2-38
    III. The Captivity of Judah . . . . Ch. 39, 52
    IV. Prophecies After the Captivity . . . . Ch. 40-51

9. **SUMMARY:**

    Jeremiah was commissioned to bring the last appeal from Jehovah to Judah before destruction came (7:2-7). He was to announce the inevitable doom that was coming upon Judah, Jerusalem, and the Temple under the hand of Nebuchadnezzar, king of Babylon (21:1-10). Jeremiah alone set the duration of the Babylonian Captivity at 70 years (25:11; 29:10). He also had a message of judgment on the Gentile nations (46-51) and foretold the coming of the glorious New Covenant (31: 31-34).

10. **CHRIST SEEN:**

    Christ is seen as the Appointed Prophet to Jerusalem, suffering with, for, and at the hands of his own nation. He is the Righteous Branch, the King, the Lord Our Righteousness, and the Maker of the New Covenant (Ch. 23, 31).

LAMENTATIONS

1. **TITLES:**

    A. Lamentations = mournings, wailings, weepings
    B. The Book of Mourning

2. **AUTHOR:**

    Written by Jeremiah, "the weeping prophet", who prophesied to the House of Judah. He also wrote the book of Jeremiah.

3. **DATE:**

    A. Jeremiah's ministry covered a period of about 66 years (626 - 560 B.C.), beginning in the reign of Josiah, continuing through the reigns of Jehoahaz, Jehoiakim, Jeconiah, and ending after the reign of Zedekiah, Judah's last king.
    B. Written about 586 B.C., shortly after the fall of Jerusalem.

4. **KEY WORDS:**

    A. Zion --- 15
    B. Afflict (ed, ion) --- 9
    C. Jerusalem -- 7
    D. Desolate (ion) --- 7

    KEY PHRASE:

    A. "The Lord hath" --- 14

5. **KEY VERSES:** 1:12; 2:17

6. **PURPOSE:**

    A. To express through the prophet in a series of lamentations the sorrow of the heart of God over Jerusalem.
    B. To record the affliction and desolation of Jerusalem.

7. **MESSAGE:**

    A. The sin of disobedience to God's Laws brings desolation and the wrath of God, even upon God's own people.
    B. Though God loves His own, and has compassion for His people, He must yet punish the willfully obstinate and disobedient.

8. **OUTLINE:**

I.	The First Poem:	Jerusalem's Plight	Ch. 1	The City
II.	The Second Poem:	Jehovah's Anger	Ch. 2	The Sanctuary
III.	The Third Poem:	Jeremiah's Sorrows	Ch. 3	The Prophet
IV.	The Fourth Poem:	Jehovah's Anger	Ch. 4	The People
V.	The Fifth Poem:	Jeremiah's Prayer	Ch. 5	The Prayer

9. **SUMMARY:**

    Lamentations consists of five poems. Chapters 1 through 4 are acrostic; each of the verses beginning successively with one of the 22 letters of the Hebrew alphabet. Each of these poems has a reference to desolation, God's judgments and sorrows, and closes with a prayer petition (except the fourth). The fifth poem is completely intercessory prayer. The Lamentations of Jeremiah concern these four things:

    A. The People of Judah
    B. The Temple of Solomon
    C. The City of Jerusalem
    D. The Land of Palestine

10. **CHRIST SEEN:**

    Christ is seen as the interceeding, weeping Prophet, "the Man of Sorrows", lamenting as He foretells the desolations of Judah, Jerusalem, the Temple, and the Land. (Lk. 19:41-44; Lk. 21:20-24; Mt. 23:37, 38; Mt. 24:1-4).

EZEKIEL

1. **TITLES:**

    A. Ezekiel = God will strengthen, the strength of God
    B. The Book of The Son of Man
    C. The Book of Visions

2. **AUTHOR:**

    Written by Ezekiel, the prophet-priest of Vision, who ministered to the House of Judah and prophesied concerning the House of Israel.

3. **DATE:**

    A. Ezekiel's ministry covered a period of about 30 years (593 - 563 B.C.), beginning the last years of Zedekiah's reign and continuing into the Babylonian Captivity.
    B. Written between 593 and 563 B.C.

4. **KEY WORDS:**

A. Blood (y)	56	D. Spirit	26	
B. Desolate (ion, ions)	47	E. Vision (s)	18	
C. Sanctuary	34			

    KEY PHRASES:

    A. "thus saith the Lord (God)" 209
    B. "son of man" 93
    C. "they shall know that I am the Lord" 63
    D. "the Word of the Lord came" 50
    E. "the glory of the Lord (or, God of Israel)" 16

5. **KEY VERSES:** 10:4, 18; 36:24-28; 43:2

6. **PURPOSE:**

    A. To declare to the unbelieving House of Judah that the temple and city would be destroyed, once the "Glory of the Lord" had departed.
    B. To show the Gentile nations their inevitable judgment.
    C. To predict the return of the "Glory of the Lord" to a new temple.

7. **MESSAGE:**

    A. When a nation departs from the "Glory of the Lord", the "Glory of the Lord" departs from it.
    B. All nations are held accountable to God and judged by Him.
    C. God is righteous to judge and merciful to restore.

8. **OUTLINE:**

    I. Judgment on Judah and Jerusalem (Pre-Seige) .... Ch. 1-24
    (The Glory Departs From the Old Temple)
    II. Judgment on the Gentile Nations (Mid-Seige) .... Ch. 25-32, 35
    III. Restoration Under Messiah (Post-Seige) .... Ch. 33-48
    (The Glory Returns To a New Temple)

9. **SUMMARY:**

    Ezekiel, as a priest, opens and closes his prophecy with visions of the Temple and the Glory departing and returning. Ezekiel is the only prophet to mention Israel's idolatry in Egypt and God's thought to destroy them for His name's sake (20:1-9). He is the only prophet to describe Lucifer's position prior to his fall under the context of the king of Tyre (28:11-19). There are also prophecies in the last section concerning Messiah's Times and Restoration under the New Covenant.

    NOTE: Much corresponds in the visions of Ezekiel and Revelation.

10. **CHRIST SEEN:**

    Christ is seen as "the Son of Man", sent to the rebellious house of Judah (2:1; Jn. 1:11), beginning his ministry to the faithful remnant at the age of 30 (1:1; Lk. 3:21-23) with opened heavens. He prophesied of the departing Glory from the material Temple at Jerusalem and its destruction (Mt. 24:1, 2), and spoke of the Glory returning to the New Temple, the Church (Eph. 2:20-22).

DANIEL

1. **TITLES:**

   A. Daniel = judgment of God, or God is my judge
   B. The Book of Judgment
   C. The Book of The Kingdoms

2. **AUTHOR:**

   Written by Daniel, the prophet of The Captivity, who prophesied concerning both earthly and heavenly Kingdoms.

3. **DATE:**

   A. Daniel's ministry covered a period of about 70 years (606 - 536 B.C.), beginning during the reign of Jehoiakim, continuing through the reigns of Jeconiah and Zedekiah of Judah, and ending during the reign of Cyrus, king of Medo-Persia.
   B. Written between 560 and 536 B.C.

4. **KEY WORDS:**

A.	King (s, 's, ly)	187	E.	Vision (s)	32
B.	Kingdom (s)	59	F.	Dream (s, ed)	29
C.	Time (s)	47	G.	End	27
D.	Interpretation (s, ing)	32	H.	Dominion (s)	19

   KEY PHRASE:

   A. "most High (rules)" -------------------------------------- 12

5. **KEY VERSES:** 2:21, 22; 7:13, 14, 18

6. **PURPOSE:**

   A. To illustrate God's care for His people even in their captivity.
   B. To prove the Kingdom of God to be higher than any earthly kingdom.
   C. To show how God controls and directs the history of the nations.

7. **MESSAGE:**

   A. The sovereignty of the "Most High God" is universal.
   B. God reveals His secrets to His servants, and does not leave them in darkness concerning His dealings among the nations.

8. **OUTLINE:**

   I. Book of History ------ (written in Chaldee) . . . . Ch. 1-6
   Dreams of Nebuchadnezzar
   II. Book of Prophecy---- (written in Hebrew) . . . . Ch. 7-12
   Visions of Daniel

9. **SUMMARY:**

   The experiences of Daniel and his companions show that the Lord's loyal and obedient servants are often blessed with earthly success, trusted with His secrets, and comforted in times of suffering and trial. The dreams of Nebuchadnezzar in the first six chapters show the kingdoms of this world from the human point of view (i.e. in the image of a deified man). The visions of Daniel in the last six chapters show the same kingdoms from the divine point of view (i.e. as wild, carnivorous beasts), giving their successive order. Undoubtedly the most comprehensive (and controversial) prophecy in Daniel is the "70 week" prophecy reaching in its time span from the close of the Babylonian Captivity to the ultimate establishment of the everlasting Kingdom of "The Son of Man".

   NOTE: Daniel and Revelation are companion volumes each complementing and completing the other.

10. **CHRIST SEEN:**

   Christ is seen as the Son of Man (7:13), the Stone cut out of the mountain without hands (2:34, 35, 44, 45), crushing the Kingdoms of this world (Mt. 21:42-44). The Kingdom of God is seen as an everlasting Kingdom (Dan. 7:27) and Christ is King of Kings and Lord of Lords (Rev. 19:16).

HOSEA

1. **TITLES:**

    A. Hosea = salvation, the Lord Saves
    B. The Book of Persevering Love
    C. The Book of Law and Love

2. **AUTHOR:**

    Written by Hosea, the prophet of Law and Love, who ministered to the House of Israel.

3. **DATE:**

    A. Hosea's ministry covered a period of about 45 years (755 - 710 B.C.), beginning at the end of the reign of Jeroboam II of Israel, continuing through the reigns of Zechariah, Shallum, Menahem, Pekah, and Hoshea, and ending after the Assyrian conquest of Israel during the reign of Hezekiah of Judah.
    B. Written between 750 and 710 B.C.

4. **KEY WORDS:**

    A. Israel --- 44
    B. Ephraim --- 37
    C. Turn (ed), Return (ed) (one Hebrew Word) -------------------- 20
    D. Whoredom (s) -- 14
    E. Mercy (ies) -- 11

5. **KEY VERSES:** 1:6, 9; 2:4, 23; 14:1, 4

6. **PURPOSE:**

    A. To call Israel to repentance.
    B. To prophesy the cause of the Assyrian Captivity, which was the unfaithfulness of Israel.
    C. To foretell the restoration which would come only through Messiah.

7. **MESSAGE:**

    A. The Lord loves and longs to restore and heal the backslider, and through chastisement and punishment of the Law, He causes such to return to Him.
    B. Love balances, but never violates Law.

8. **OUTLINE:**

    I.   The Prophet -- The Symbolic Marriage . . . . Ch. 1-3
         A.   The Prophet's Family . . . . Ch. 1
         B.   The Unfaithful Wife . . . . Ch. 2
         C.   The Faithful Redeeming Husband . . . . Ch. 3
    II. The Prophecy -- The Word of the Lord . . . . Ch. 4-14
         A.   Israel's Sin ---------------------------------- God is Holy . . . . Ch. 4-7
         B.   Israel's Punishment -------------------- God is Just . . . . Ch. 8-10
         C.   Israel's Restoration --------------------- God is Love . . . . Ch. 11-14

9. **SUMMARY:**

    The Book of Hosea sets forth Hosea's domestic life as an example of God's dealings with Israel, revealing His union with the nation, their unfaithfulness to the marriage covenant, His chastisement of her, and His love and mercy in redeeming and restoring her to Himself. It also shows the relationship between three great covenants.

    A. Abrahamic Covenant ---------------------- The Nation Chosen
    B. Mosaic Covenant ----------------------------- The Nation Chastised
    C. New Covenant --------------------------------- The Nation Cleansed

10. **CHRIST SEEN:**

    Christ is seen as The Prophet, (Acts 3:22, 23) fulfilling the law (Mt. 5:17, 18) and redeeming in love (Jn. 3:16).

JOEL

1. **TITLES:**

    A.   Joel = Jehovah is God; that wills, commands, or swears
    B.   The Book of the Day of the Lord

2. **AUTHOR:**

    Written by Joel, the prophet of Pentecost, who ministered to the House of Judah.

3. **DATE:**

    A.   Joel's ministry probably covered a period of about 30 years (810 - 780 B.C.), during the reigns of Joash, Amaziah, and Uzziah of Judah.
    B.   Written between 810 and 780 B.C.

4. **KEY WORDS:**

A.	Great	10	D.	Gather	6
B.	Zion	7	E.	Judah	6
C.	Wine	7	F.	Offering	6

    KEY PHRASE:

    A.   "the day of the Lord" ---------------------- 5

5. **KEY VERSES:** 2:28-32

6. **PURPOSE:**

    (A three-fold application of "the day of the Lord")

    A.   Local: To call the House of Judah, which was under Divine judgments, to repentance.
    B.   Prophetical: To point to the last days judgments, repentance, revival, and outpouring of the Spirit upon all flesh.
    C.   Final: To point to The Day of the Second Coming of the Lord.

    NOTE: The day of the Lord runs throughout the history of the Kingdom of God, occurring in each particular judgment as a type of that Great and Final Day of the Lord.

7. **MESSAGE:**

    A.   True repentance is a Godly sorrow, a rending of the heart, and a turning from evil.
    B.   True repentance lays at the foundation of all real revival and every outpouring of the Spirit.

8. **OUTLINE:**

    I.   Ruin and Repentance ----------------------- Judgment . . . . Ch. 1:1-2:17   (Historical)
        A.   Ruin . . . . Ch. 1:1-2:11
        B.   Repentance . . . . Ch. 2:12-17
    II.   Revival and Restoration ------------------- Blessing . . . . Ch. 2:18-3:21   (Prophetical)
        A.   Revival . . . . Ch. 2:18-32
        B.   Restoration . . . . Ch. 3:1-21

9. **SUMMARY:**

    Joel gives us a picture of Judah living in the land promised to Abraham and his seed. They were receiving the curse of the Palestinian Covenant (Deut. 29:1) by breaking it's conditions of blessing (Deut. 11:10-17; I Kings 8:35-40). The Word of the Lord through Joel calls them to genuine repentance; an inward rending of the heart and not an outward rending of the garments. The Lord promises the nation of Judah refreshing, revival, and restoration through a natural out-poured rain, which shadowed and prophesied of the outpouring of spiritual rain upon the church. This promised outpouring of the Holy Spirit is Joel's distinctive link with the New Testament (Acts 2:14-21). Thus he is called 'The Prophet of Pentecost".

10. **CHRIST SEEN:**

    Christ is seen as our "Jehovah-God", the Promiser of (Lk. 24:49), the Receiver of (Acts 2: 2:33), and the Baptizer in (Jn. 1:31-33) the out-poured Spirit.

AMOS

1. **TITLES:**

   A. Amos = burden bearer, or bearing a load
   B. The Book of Judgment
   C. The Book of Punishment

2. **AUTHOR:**

   Written by Amos, the prophet of Punishment, who ministered to the House of Israel.

3. **DATE:**

   A. Amos' ministry covered a period of about 10 years (765 - 755 B.C.), during the reign of Jeroboam II of Israel.
   B. Written between 765 and 755 B.C.

4. **KEY WORDS:**

   A. Israel --- 30
   B. Captive (ity) -- 13
   C. Transgress (ion, ions) -- 12
   D. Punish (ment) --- 9

   KEY PHRASES:

   A. "I will not turn away the punishment thereof" --------------------- 8
   B. "yet have ye not returned unto me" ------------------------------- 5

5. **KEY VERSES:** 4:11, 12

6. **PURPOSE:**

   A. To pronounce punishment upon The Gentile nations for their transgressions.
   B. To pronounce punishment upon Israel, the chosen nation, for their transgressions.
   C. To proclaim promises of restoration in Messianic times.

7. **MESSAGE:**

   A. God is sovereign over all nations and holds them accountable for their treatment of other races and nations.
   B. National sin brings national punishment.

8. **OUTLINE:**

   I. Eight Burdens On Gentile Nations and Israel .... Ch. 1-2
      (Announcement/Sentence/Sins)
   II. Three Discourses Against Israel .... Ch. 3-6
      (Judgment Deserved/Judgment Decreed)
   III. Five Visions Concerning Israel .... Ch. 7-9
      (Judgment Restrained/Judgment Determined/Judgment Executed)

9. **SUMMARY:**

   Amos was a herdsman and was not educated in the schools of the prophets, neither was he of the priestly or kingly lines. Nevertheless he was chosen to be a prophet of Divine justice, upholding the righteousness of the law, and declaring judgments upon the sinful nations. His ministry deals particularly with the relationships between nations, denouncing their sins of inhumanity. Amos also gives the notable prophecy of the restoration of the Tabernacle of David and the Gentiles coming into blessing under Messiah's times (Acts 15:15-18).

10. **CHRIST SEEN:**

    Christ is seen as our "Burden-Bearer", not only bearing our sins (Is. 53:12), but also the burden of the Word of the Lord (Jn. 1:1, 2). He is the final Judge and Punisher of all nations (II Thes. 1:7-9) and he is the Builder of the church (Mt. 16:18, 19), the spiritual Tabernacle of David.

OBADIAH

1. **TITLES:**

   A.   Obadiah = servant of the Lord, or worshipper of Jehovah
   B.   The Book of Retribution

2. **AUTHOR:**

   Written by Obadiah, the prophet of Divine Retribution, who prophesied against Edom.

3. **DATE:**

   A.   Obadiah's ministry covered a period of about 8 years (848 - 840 B.C.), during the reign of Jehoram of Judah. (Some place Obadiah's ministry during or after the Babylonian Captivity.)
   B.   Probably written between 848 and 840 B.C.

4. **KEY WORDS:**

   A.   Day --- 12
   B.   Esau, Edom --- 9
   C.   Possess (ions) --- 7

   KEY PHRASE:

   A.   "cut off" --- 3

5. **KEY VERSES:** 4, 15

6. **PURPOSE:**

   A.   To pronounce doom, destruction, and desolation on Esau/Edom.
   B.   To confirm the promises of the deliverance and restoration of Jacob/Israel both historically and prophetically.

7. **MESSAGE:**

   A.   "Pride goeth before destruction, and an haughty spirit before a fall" (Pr. 16:18).
   B.   "As a man soweth so shall he also reap" (Gal. 6:7-9).

8. **OUTLINE:**

   I.   Esau/Edom . . . . Vs. 1-16
        A.   Destruction Decided . . . . Vs. 1-9
        B.   Sins Denounced . . . . Vs. 10-14
        C.   Judgments Declared . . . . Vs. 15-16
   II. Jacob/Israel . . . . Vs. 17-21
        Deliverance and Restoration

9. **SUMMARY:**

   The book of Obadiah shows The Law of Divine Retribution.

   > "as thou hast done . . . so it shall be done unto thee" (v. 15)

   - Edom's treachery against Judah
     -- Edom to perish through treachery (v. 11)
   - Edom robbed Judah (V. 13)
     -- Edom to be robbed (V. 5, 6)
   - Edom lifted sword in violence (V. 10)
     -- Edom to have sword in violence (V. 9)
   - Edom sought utter destruction of Judah (V. 12-14)
     -- Edom to have utter destruction (V. 9, 10, 18)

   Though Judah was promised restoration after punishment, Edom was given no promise of restoration. The background and key to this book is to be found in the relationship of these two nations and their fathers, Esau and Jacob.

   NOTE: There are several cross references between Obadiah and Amos.

10. **CHRIST SEEN:**

    Christ is seen as the Servant (Phil. 2:7) and Worshipper (Heb 2:12) of Jehovah, and the Executor of Divine Retribution (II Thes. 1:6-10).

JONAH

1. **TITLES:**

   A. Jonah = dove
   B. The Book of Mercy On The Gentiles

2. **AUTHOR:**

   Written by Jonah, the prophet of Mercy On The Gentiles, who ministered to the House of Israel and to Assyria.

3. **DATE:**

   A. Jonah's ministry covered a period of about 15 years (785 - 770 B.C.), during the reigns of Jehoash and Jeroboam II of Israel.
   B. Written between 780 and 770 B.C.

4. **KEY WORDS:**

   A. Anger (ry) --- 6
   B. Prepared --- 4
   C. Down --- 4

   KEY PHRASE:

   A. "presence of the Lord" -- 3

5. **KEY VERSES:** 3:2, 10

6. **PURPOSE:**

   A. To demonstrate God's love and mercy for the Gentiles as well as for Israel (Rom. 3:29; 10:12).
   B. To show God's method of dealing with His disobedient servants.
   C. To set forth Messiah's ministry typologically.

7. **MESSAGE:**

   A. "God is no respecter of persons: But in every nation he that feareth Him, and worketh righteousness, is accepted with Him." (Acts 10:34, 35)
   B. God's servants must learn the lesson that God will have mercy on whom He will have mercy.
   C. Through disobedience, the servant of God will bring the chastening of God upon himself.

8. **OUTLINE:**

   I.   Jonah and the Storm --------- Disobedient Prophet . . . . Ch. 1
   II.   Jonah and the Fish ----------- Praying Prophet . . . . Ch. 2
   III. Jonah and the City ----------- Preaching Prophet . . . . Ch. 3
   IV.   Jonah and the Lord ---------- Chastened Prophet . . . . Ch. 4

9. **SUMMARY:**

   In Jonah, we find the great Gentile city of Nineveh repenting and turning to God under the reluctant preaching of the prophet Jonah. In chapter one we see Jonah fleeing from the presence of the Lord, going down to Joppa, down into the ship, and finally down into the belly of the fish which God had prepared. Then in chapter two he prays to God and is delivered from the fish. In chapter three Jonah finally delivers God's message to Nineveh and the whole city repents, but in chapter four he is once again chastened by the Lord for being angry when God does not fulfill Jonah's prophecy by destroying Nineveh.

10. **CHRIST SEEN:**

   Christ is seen as "the Greater than Jonah" using Jonah's experience as a sign of his own death, burial, and resurrection and of God's mercy on the repentant Gentiles (Mt. 12:39-41).

MICAH

1. **TITLES:**

   A. Micah = who is like Jehovah, God-like
   B. The Book of Sermons
   C. The Book of Conviction

2. **AUTHOR**

   Written by Micah, the prophet of Messianic Conviction, who ministered to both Israel and Judah. (He was the only "minor" prophet to do so.)

3. **DATE:**

   A. Micah's ministry covered a period of about 35 years (735 - 700 B.C.), during the reigns of Jotham, Ahaz, and Hezekiah of Judah and the reigns of Pekah and Hoshea of Israel. Thus he witnessed the Captivity of Israel to Assyria.
   B. Written between 735 and 700 B.C.

4. **KEY WORDS:**

A.	Israel	12	E.	Sin (s, ed)		7
B.	Hear (d)	10	F.	Transgression (s)		6
C.	Zion	9	G.	Gather, Assemble		6
D.	Jerusalem	8	H.	Remnant		6

5. **KEY VERSES:** 3:8; 6:8; 7:18

6. **PURPOSE:**

   A. To convict Israel and Judah of their sin and to show their subsequent judgments in their respective captivities to Assyria and Babylon.
   B. To give to the faithful remnant promises of restoration in Messiah's times.
   C. To pinpoint the city of Messiah's birth. (Micah is the only prophet to do so.)

7. **MESSAGE:**

   A. God hates transgression and ritualism, and after dealing with them, delights in pardon.
   B. Those who remain faithful can be assured of God's mercy and redeeming grace.

8. **OUTLINE:**

   I. Sin and Judgment . . . . Ch. 1-3
   To the People ---------------- "Hear Ye"
   II. Grace and Restoration . . . . Ch. 4, 5
   To the Leaders -------------- "Hear Ye"
   III. Controversy and Comfort . . . . Ch. 6, 7
   To the Mountains ---------- "Hear Ye"

9. **SUMMARY:**

   The prophecy of Micah consists of several "sermons" intermingled with warnings, judgments, exhortations, promises of restoration and Messianic predictions. In the first sermon to the people he witnesses to Israel and Judah concerning their apostasy from God and their subsequent judgments. In his second sermon to the leaders he consols Israel and Judah with distinctive Messianic promises of restoration, then in the third sermon to the mountains (kingdoms) he pleads with Israel concerning the essence of true religion and closes with the comforting words that God will pardon.

10. **CHRIST SEEN:**

   Christ is seen as the Heavenly Micah, who is "like God"; born in Bethlehem (5:2; Mt. 2:1-6), rejected as the King of the Jews (5:1; Jn. 19:15), and the Establisher of His House (4:1, 2; Heb. 3:6).

NAHUM

1. **TITLES:**

   A. Nahum = comforter, or penitent
   B. The Book of <u>Vengeance</u>

2. **AUTHOR:**

   Written by <u>Nahum</u>, the prophet of <u>Comfort and Vengeance</u>, who ministered to the House of <u>Judah</u> and to the city of <u>Nineveh</u>.

3. **DATE:**

   A. Nahum's ministry covered a period of about 30 years (650 - 620 B.C.), during the reigns of Manasseh, Amon, and Josiah of Judah.
   B. Written between 650 and 620 B.C.

4. **KEY WORDS:**

   A. Against --- 5
   B. Wicked (ness) --- 4
   C. Flee (th) -- 4
   D. Away --- 4
   E. Vengeance, Revengeth -- 3
   F. Afflict -- 3

5. **KEY VERSES:** 1:2, 3

6. **PURPOSE:**

   A. To pronounce the judgment of God's vengeance upon Nineveh.
   B. To comfort Judah by declaring the destruction of her enemies.

7. **MESSAGE:**

   A. God is against those who are against Him.
   B. Divine vengeance comes upon those who reject God's mercy.
   C. God's only recourse with a hardened apostate nation is to destroy it.

8. **OUTLINE:**

   I.   Judgment <u>Declared</u> ---------- God Avenges . . . . Ch. 1
   II.   Judgment <u>Described</u> -------- How God Avenges . . . . Ch. 2
   III. Judgment <u>Deserved</u> ---------- Why God Avenges . . . . Ch. 3

9. **SUMMARY:**

   Nineveh, the capital of Assyria, had the ministry of two prophets, Jonah and Nahum. Jonah was a prophet of mercy, calling the city to repentance. At that time Nineveh repented and was spared from the destruction prophesied by Jonah. In the 150 years following its repentance, the city lapsed back into idolatry worse than before. Thus Nahum was sent to Nineveh to announce the vengeance of God in the soon-coming destruction of the city. Assyria, after being shown God's mercy, showed no mercy to Israel in the Assyrian Captivity and thus God rendered to them judgment without mercy (Jas. 2:13). Nahum's declaration of Divine vengeance upon Nineveh was a comfort to Judah.

10. **CHRIST SEEN:**

    Christ is seen as <u>The Prophet of Comfort and Vengeance,</u> comforting His own (Jn. 14:16) and "executing vengeance on all them that know not God and obey not the gospel of our Lord Jesus Christ" (II Thes. 1:8).

HABAKKUK

1. **TITLES:**

   A. Habakkuk = embrace of love, wrestler
   B. The Book of Faith

2. **AUTHOR:**

   Written by Habakkuk, the prophet of Faith, who ministered to the House of Judah.

3. **DATE:**

   A. Habakkuk's ministry covered a period of about 20 years (620 - 600 B.C.), during the reigns of Josiah, Jehoahaz, and Jehoiakim of Judah.
   B. Written between 620 and 600 B.C.

4. **KEY WORDS:**

   A. Violence -- 6
   B. Woe -- 5
   C. Judgment --- 4
   D. Spoil (ed, ing) -- 4

5. **KEY VERSE:** 2:4

6. **PURPOSE:**

   A. To set forth the problem as to why a Holy God would use the much more wicked nation of Babylon to judge the wicked nation of Judah.
   B. To answer the problem by revealing that God will in turn judge Babylon.

7. **MESSAGE:**

   A. God is consistent with Himself in view of permitted evil.
   B. God is holy and righteous and must punish sin.
   C. The just shall live by faith.

8. **OUTLINE:**

   I.   The Burden: The Problem of Faith -------- First Conversation . . . . . . Ch. 1
   II.   The Vision: The Answer of Faith ---------- Second Conversation . . . . . Ch. 2
   III. The Prayer: The Assurance of Faith ------ Prophet's Psalm . . . . Ch. 3

9. **SUMMARY:**

   Habakkuk is not a direct address to the people of Judah, but rather is a dialogue between the prophet and God. In the first conversation, he complains of God's apparent lack of concern over Judah's sin. The Lord replies that He will use the Babylonians to judge Judah. To Habakkuk this only complicates the matter and in the second conversation he complains of God's apparent lack of concern over the cruelty of the Babylonians, and the Lord answers that He will also judge Babylon for her violence. The prophet, having his questions answered, closes with a psalm of trust and triumph in the Lord.

   NOTE: This book contains the only positive use of the word faith in the Old Testament.

10. **CHRIST SEEN:**

   Christ is seen as The Judge of Babylon (Rev. 17, 18) and the Rewarder of those that diligently seek Him in faith (Heb. 10:38; 11:6).

ZEPHANIAH

1. TITLES:

    A.   Zephaniah = hidden of Jehovah, Jehovah has concealed, or protected

    B.   The Book of The Day of Wrath

2. AUTHOR:

    Written by Zephaniah, the prophet of The Day of Wrath, who ministered to the House of Judah.

3. DATE:

    A.   Zephaniah's ministry covered a period of about 14 years (638 - 624 B.C.), during the reign of Josiah, King of Judah.

    B.   Written between 638 and 624 B.C.

4. KEY WORDS:

    A.   Day -- 21

    B.   Desolate (ion) --- 8

    C.   Against -- 8

    D.   Anger, Wrath --- 6

    E.   Remnant -- 4

KEY PHRASES:

    A.   "I will (he, Lord)" --- 30

    B.   "day of the Lord" --- 7

    C.   "cut off" -- 5

5. KEY VERSE: 1:18

6. PURPOSE:

    A.   To warn the House of Judah of the coming day of wrath: Their desolation at the hand of Babylon.

    B.   To warn Philistia, Moab, Ammon, Ethiopia, and Nineveh of the coming day of wrath.

    C.   To comfort the faithful remnant with promises of restoration.

7. MESSAGE:

    A.   "Righteousness exalteth a nation but sin is a reproach to any people." (Pr. 14:34)

    B.   God Himself will punish nations for their wickedness.

8. OUTLINE:

    I.   The Day of Wrath upon Judah . . . . Ch. 1:1-2:3   (Look Within)

    II.   The Day of Wrath on the Nations . . . . Ch. 2:4-15   (Look Around)

    III. Reason for Wrath upon Judah . . . . Ch. 3:1-7   (Look Above)

    IV. Faithful Remnant Restored . . . . Ch. 3:8-20   (Look Beyond)

9. SUMMARY:

    Both Zephaniah the prophet and Josiah the king were great, great grandsons of Hezekiah (1:1). Thus Zephaniah was a prince of the royal house of David. His prophecy reflects the evil times begun under the reigns of Manasseh and Amon. He therefore sees the coming day of the Lord as being a day of wrath, anger, trouble, distress, desolation, darkness, and gloominess. This had a historical and local fulfillment in the desolations under Babylon, during which God preserved unto Himself a faithful remnant. His prophecy also points prophetically and ultimately to the Second Coming of the Lord Jesus Christ, and the preservation of the Church.

10. CHRIST SEEN:

    Christ is seen as a Jealous God (1:18; 3:8; II Cor. 11:2) in relation to His people, and the Executor of God's judgments (Jn. 5:27) in the day of wrath (Rom. 2:5, 6).

HAGGAI

1. **TITLES:**

    A. Haggai = festive, or my feast
    B. The Book of the Rebuilding of the Temple

2. **AUTHOR:**

    Written by Haggai, the prophet of The Temple, who ministered to the restored House of Judah; especially Zerubbabel and Jeshua.

3. **DATE:**

    A. Haggai's ministry covered a period of about 15 years (520 - 505 B.C.), beginning 16 years after the first remnant returned from Babylon.
    B. Written in 520 B.C.

4. **KEY WORDS:**

    A. Day --- 11
    B. House (of the Lord) ----------------------------------- 8
    C. Consider -- 5

    KEY PHRASES:

    A. "saith the Lord" ------------------------------------- 19
    B. "Lord of hosts" -------------------------------------- 14

5. **KEY VERSE:** 1:8

6. **PURPOSE:**

    A. To encourage the leaders (Zerubbabel the governor and Jeshua the high priest) and the first remnant that had returned under Zerubbabel to rebuild the temple.
    B. To point toward Messiah's times.

7. **MESSAGE:**

    A. God and His House must be first in the life and service of the redeemed.
    B. God will bless those who put Him first (Mt. 6:33).

8. **OUTLINE:**

    I.   The Word of Rebuke . . . . Ch. 1:1-15
         To Zerubbabel, Jeshua, and the people
    II. The Word of Encouragement . . . . Ch. 2:1-9
         To Zerubbabel and Jeshua
    III. The Word of Correction . . . . Ch. 2:10-19
         To the Priests
    IV. The Word of Promise . . . . Ch. 2:20-23
         To Zerubbabel

9. **SUMMARY:**

    Haggai was the first of the three prophets to minister to Judah after the Babylonian Captivity. Because of opposition, the work of rebuilding the temple had ceased for several years. The people had grown cold-hearted and had not made any attempt to begin the work again. Thus Haggai and Zechariah exhorted them to do so. The bulk of Haggai's prophecy is personal, to Zerubbabel the governor (political leader) and to Jeshua the high priest (religious leader). The remainder contains rebuke and encouragement to the priests and the people. Interwoven among the prophecies concerning the literal temple are prophecies pertaining to the spiritual temple -- the Church.

10. **CHRIST SEEN:**

    Christ is seen as our Prophet (Haggai), Priest (Jeshua), and Prince (Zerubbabel), thus uniting the three offices in one person. He is the Builder of The Lord's House -- The Church (Mt. 16:18, Heb. 3:5).

ZECHARIAH

1. **TITLES:**

   A. Zechariah = Jehovah remembers
   B. The Book of Messianic Visions

2. **AUTHOR:**

   Written by Zechariah, the prophet of Messianic Vision, who ministered to the restored house of Judah.

3. **DATE:**

   A. Zechariah's ministry covered a period of about 40 years (520 - 480 B.C.), beginning 16 years after the first remnant returned from Babylon.
   B. Chapters 1-8 were written between 520 and 518 B.C., while chapters 9-14 were written between 490 and 480 B.C.

4. **KEY WORDS:**

   A. Jerusalem -- 41
   B. Judah -- 22
   C. Against -- 18
   D. House (of the Lord) -- 10
   E. Jealous -- 5

   KEY PHRASES:

   A. "Lord of hosts" -- 53
   B. "saith the Lord" --- 42
   C. "that day" --- 21
   D. "word of the Lord" --- 13

5. **KEY VERSES:** 6:12, 13; 8:1-3

6. **PURPOSE:**

   A. To stir the remnant to complete the unfinished temple. (Similar to Haggai.)
   B. To prophesy of the Messiah in His first and second comings and the establishment of His Kingdom.

7. **MESSAGE:**

   A. God is jealous for His House and will see to it that it is restored.
   B. All of God's purposes are consummated in Messiah and His Kingdom.

8. **OUTLINE:**

   I.   Eight Symbolic Visions . . . . Ch. 1-6
   II. Four Didactic Messages . . . . Ch. 7-8
   III. Two Prophetic Burdens . . . . Ch. 9-14

9. **SUMMARY:**

   Zechariah was the second of the three prophets to minister to Judah after the Babylonian Captivity. The nature of Haggai's message was one of rebuke dealing with the outward work of rebuilding the temple, while Zechariah's message was one of encouragement to bring about an inward spiritual change in the people. Thus we see them ministering together (Ezra 5:1). The first two sections of Zechariah were given while the temple was being rebuilt and are partially fulfilled at that time. The third section was given after the temple was rebuilt and overflows into Messianic times.

   NOTE: There are more specific Messianic predictions in Zechariah than in all the other "minor prophets" combined.

10. **CHRIST SEEN:**

    Christ is seen as the "One Whom Jehovah Remembers" (Zechariah), as the Branch (3:8, Mt. 2:23 -- Nazarene), Jehovah's Servant (3:8; Phil. 2:7), the Smitten Shepherd (13:7; Mk. 14:27), the King-Priest (6:9-12; Heb. 5:5, 6), the Builder of the spiritual Temple (6:12-15; Mt. 16:18), and the King over all the earth (14:9; Rev. 19:16).

MALACHI

1. **TITLES:**

   A. Malachi = messenger of Jehovah, or my messenger
   B. The Book of The Lord's Messengers

2. **AUTHOR:**

   Written by Malachi, the Prophet of The Lord's Messengers, who was the last Old Testament prophet to minister to the restored House of Judah.

3. **DATE:**

   A. Malachi's ministry covered a period of about 25 years (435 - 410 B.C.), during the governorship of Nehemiah over the restored House of Judah.
   B. Written between 435 and 410 B.C. This was the last Old Testament book to be written.

4. **KEY WORDS:**

   A. Where? (in, fore), What? --- 13
   B. Curse (d) -- 7
   C. Covenant -- 6
   D. Treacherously --- 5

   KEY PHRASES:

   A. "saith the Lord" --- 25
   B. "Lord of hosts" -- 24
   C. "ye say" --- 11

5. **KEY VERSES:** 3:1, 9, 10

6. **PURPOSE:**

   A. To reprove the remnant for their neglect of the temple.
   B. To reprove the priests for their profaning of the temple worship.
   C. To encourage the faithful remnant with Messianic promises.

7. **MESSAGE:**

   A. Sins of hypocrisy harden and blind the heart.
   B. Obedience brings blessing and disobedience brings cursing.

8. **OUTLINE:**

   I.   Message to the Priests (Religious) . . . . Ch. 1:1-2:9
   II. Message to the People (Social) . . . . Ch. 2:10-17
   III. Message to the Faithful (Moral) . . . . Ch. 3-4

9. **SUMMARY:**

   Malachi was the last of the three prophets to minister to Judah after the Babylonian Captivity. Haggai and Zechariah were sent to rebuke the people for failing to rebuild the temple. Then generations later Malachi was sent to reprove the priests and the people for their neglect, profanity, and formalism relative to the temple worship. This he did with the question and answer method (there are no less than 23 questions in this book). Malachi was the last messenger of the O.T. prophets, referring to the priests as messengers of the Lord (2:7), and pointing to the first N.T. messenger, John the Baptist (3:la; Mk. 1:2), and also to Messiah, The Messenger of the New Covenant (3:lb).

   NOTE: Between Malachi and John the Baptist come the "400 silent years".

10. **CHRIST SEEN:**

   Christ is seen as The Messenger of the New Covenant, the Refiner and Purifier of His people (3:1-3; Mt. 3:11) and the Cleanser of the temple (Jn. 2:13-17; Mt. 21:12-14).

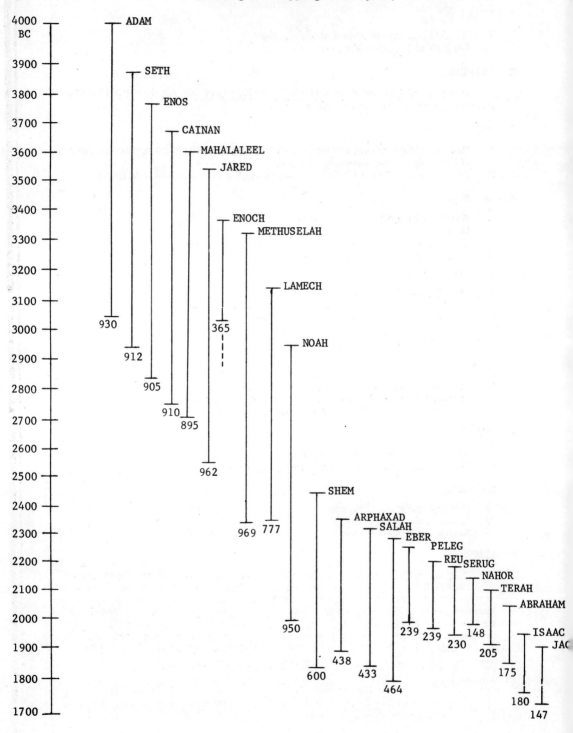

THE MINISTRIES OF THE PROPHETS
(Showing Contemporary Writing Prophets)

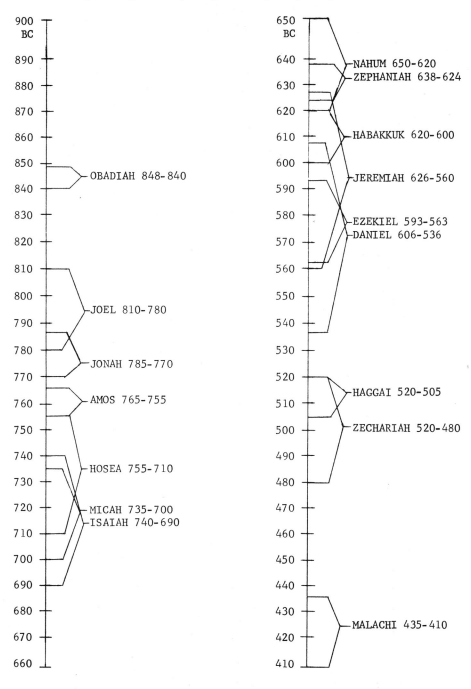

900 BC

890

880

870

860

850
— OBADIAH 848-840

840

830

820

810

800
—JOEL 810-780

790

780

770
— JONAH 785-770

760
— AMOS 765-755

750

740

730
— HOSEA 755-710

720
— MICAH 735-700
— ISAIAH 740-690

710

700

690

680

670

660

650 BC

640
—NAHUM 650-620
—ZEPHANIAH 638-624

630

620

610
—HABAKKUK 620-600

600

590
—JEREMIAH 626-560

580
—EZEKIEL 593-563
—DANIEL 606-536

570

560

550

540

530

520
—HAGGAI 520-505

510

500
—ZECHARIAH 520-480

490

480

470

460

450

440

430
—MALACHI 435-410

420

410

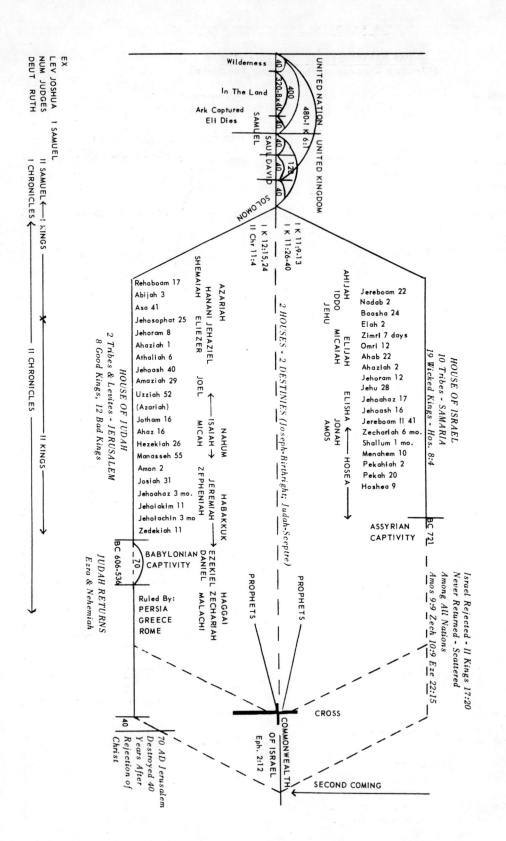

KINGDOM OF ISRAEL

EX
LEV   JOSHUA   I SAMUEL
NUM   JUDGES   II SAMUEL ←— I KINGS
DEUT RUTH   I CHRONICLES

I CHRONICLES ————— II CHRONICLES
————— I KINGS —————
————— II KINGS —————

Wilderness
In The Land
Ark Captured
Eli Dies

SAMUEL
SAUL DAVID
SOLOMON

UNITED NATION   UNITED KINGDOM

40
320-8x40
400
480-I 6:1
40
40
12x
40

I K 11:9-13
I K 11:26-40
I K 12:15,24
II Chr 11:4

HOUSE OF ISRAEL
10 Tribes - SAMARIA
19 Wicked Kings - Hos. 8:4

AHIJAH
IDDO
MICAIAH
JEHU

ELIJAH
ELISHA
JONAH
HOSEA
AMOS

Jereboam 22
Nadab 2
Baasha 24
Elah 2
Zimri 7 days
Omri 12
Ahab 22
Ahaziah 2
Jehoram 12
Jehu 28
Jehoahaz 17
Jehoash 16
Jeroboam II 41
Zechariah 6 mo.
Shallum 1 mo.
Menahem 10
Pekahiah 2
Pekah 20
Hoshea 9

ASSYRIAN
CAPTIVITY   BC 721

Israel Rejected - II Kings 17:20
Never Returned - Scattered
Among All Nations
Amos 9:9 Zech 10:9 Eze 22:15

2 HOUSES - 2 DESTINIES (Joseph-Birthright; Judah-Sceptre)

AZARIAH
HANANI JEHAZIEL
SHEMAIAH ELIEZER

JOEL

NAHUM
ISAIAH →
MICAH
ZEPHENIAH

HABAKKUK
JEREMIAH
EZEKIEL
DANIEL

HAGGAI
ZECHARIAH
MALACHI

Rehoboam 17
Abijah 3
Asa 41
Jehosophat 25
Jehoram 8
Ahaziah 1
Athaliah 6
Jehoash 40
Amaziah 29
Uzziah 52
(Azariah)
Jotham 16
Ahaz 16
Hezekiah 26
Manasseh 55
Amon 2
Josiah 31
Jehoahaz 3 mo.
Jehoiakim 11
Jehoiachin 3 mo
Zedekiah 11

HOUSE OF JUDAH
2 Tribes & Levites - JERUSALEM
8 Good Kings, 12 Bad Kings

BABYLONIAN
CAPTIVITY   BC 606-536
— 70 —

JUDAH RETURNS
Ezra & Nehemiah

Ruled By:
PERSIA
GREECE
ROME

PROPHETS

PROPHETS

PROPHETS

CROSS
COMMONWEALTH
OF ISRAEL
Eph. 2:12

70 AD Jerusalem
Destroyed 40
Years After
Rejection of
Christ
40

SECOND COMING

THE KINGS AND PROPHETS OF ISRAEL AND JUDAH

UNITED KINGDOM

Saul.......1051-1011 BC....40 Years
David......1011- 971 BC....40 Years
Solomon.... 971- 931 BC....40 Years

DIVIDED KINGDOM

KINGS OF JUDAH	BEGAN TO REIGN	YEARS	PROPHETS	KINGS OF ISRAEL	BEGAN TO REIGN	YEARS	PROPHETS
Rehoboam	931 BC	17	Shemaiah	Jeroboam	931 BC	22	Ahijah
			Iddo				Man of God
Abijam	913 BC	3	Iddo				Iddo
Asa	911 BC	41	Azariah	Nadab	910 BC	2	
			Hanani	Baasha	909 BC	24	Jehu
Jehoshaphat	873 BC	25	Jehaziel	Elah	886 BC	2	
			Eliezer	Zimri	885 BC	7days	
Jehoram	853 BC	8	Obadiah?	Omri	885 BC	12	Elijah
Ahaziah	841 BC	1		Ahab	874 BC	22	Elijah
Athaliah	841 BC	6					Micaiah
Jehoash	835 BC	40	Joel	Ahaziah	853 BC	2	Elijah
Amaziah	796 BC	29	Joel	Jehoram	852 BC	12	Elisha
Uzziah	790 BC	52	Joel	Jehu	841 BC	28	Elisha
			Isaiah	Jehoahaz	814 BC	17	Elisha
Jotham	750 BC	16	Isaiah	Jehoash	798 BC	16	Elisha
			Micah				Jonah
Ahaz	735 BC	16	Isaiah	Jeroboam II	793 BC	41	Jonah
			Micah				Amos
Hezekiah	715 BC	29	Isaiah				Hosea
			Micah	Zechariah	753 BC	6mo.	Hosea
Manasseh	695 BC	55	Nahum	Shallum	753 BC	1mo.	Hosea
Amon	642 BC	2	Nahum	Menahem	752 BC	10	Hosea
Josiah	640 BC	31	Nahum	Pekahiah	742 BC	2	Hosea
			Zephaniah	Pekah	752 BC	20	Hosea
			Habakkuk				Micah
			Jeremiah	Hoshea	732 BC	9	Hosea
			Huldah				Micah
Jehoahaz	609 BC	3mo.	Habakkuk				
			Jeremiah				
Jehoiakim	609 BC	11	Habakkuk				
			Jeremiah				
			Daniel				
Jehoiachin	597 BC	3mo.	Jeremiah				
			Daniel				
Zedekiah	597 BC	11	Jeremiah				
			Ezekiel				
			Daniel				

THE ASSYRIAN CAPTIVITY

In 721 BC the northern House of Israel was overthrown by the armies of Assyria, led by Shalmaneser. He came against Samaria, and after a siege of three years took the city, carried away Israel into Assyria, and repopulated the area.

THE BABYLONIAN CAPTIVITY

In 606 BC the southern House of Judah was overthrown by the Babylonians, led by Nebuchadnezzar. He carried out the captivity in three stages under Jehoiakim, Jehoiachin, and Zedekiah.

THE DISPERSION

Israel never returned from captivity but was scattered among the nations.

THE RESTORATION

Judah's return from captivity took place in three stages under Zerubbabel, Ezra, and Nehemiah. The prophets of this period were Haggai, Zechariah, and Malachi.